The Wonders
of Dan yr Ogof

Sarah Symons

dinas

The Wonders
of Dan yr Ogof

Sarah Symons

Dinas is an imprint of Y Lolfa

Published and printed in Wales
by Y Lolfa Cyf., Talybont, Ceredigion SY24 5AP
e-mail ylolfa@ylolfa.com
website www.ylolfa.com
tel. (01970) 832 304
fax 832 782
isdn 832 813

The Wonders
of Dan yr Ogof

Contents

Acknowledgments

I extend my heartfelt thanks to Mr Ashford Price, family and loyal staff of Dan yr Ogof for their generous hospitality and assistance during my months of research and for giving me unlimited access to photograph all the attractions, also my additional thanks to Mr Price for contributing key photographs. Thanks to the Archaeological Department of The University College of Wales, Aberystwyth, for putting me on the 'right road' with research, and to the Librarians of Brecon and Swansea Reference Libraries and to the Editor and Librarian of *The Evening Post* for their valuable assistance during that period.

I should also like to thank the Secretary and members of The South Wales Caving Club for their kind hospitality and valuable assistance in giving me access to their library, with special thanks to Mrs Elsie Little, custodian of the Alan Coase picture collection and to Mrs Coase and Messrs Andy Freem and Tony Baker of the Caving Club for contributing some of their outstanding photographs of the explored caverns. Also my special thanks to the Department of Archaeology and Numismatics at The National Museum of Wales, Cardiff, for their valuable assistance and for providing me with the photographs of the Bronze Age and Roman relics in their possession. Also I thank the Editor of *The Observer* for the photographs of the 1966 exploration which were published in the *Observer's* Colour Magazine at that time.

I would also like to include the late Miss Brenda Morgan, daughter of one of the original explorers, Mr Thomas Ashwell Morgan, in these acknowledgements, for sharing her memories of those early days with me despite her being in poor health.

Sarah Symons

Introduction and the Discovery in 1912

Reconstruction of the 1912 discovery

In 1999 Dan yr Ogof celebrated its Diamond Jubilee, and since its main show cave was opened to the public in August, 1939, its natural formations have thrilled us all with their spectacular displays. The distinctive features of Ogof-yr-Esgyrn (Bone Cave) and the Cathedral Showcave have also contributed to Dan yr Ogof's continuing success.

After the introduction of outside attractions like the Dinosaur Park, Model Iron Age Village, Shire Horse Centre and Farm, the Dan yr Ogof Complex is now Wales's top tourist attraction and ranks among the top twenty in Britain, with visitors coming here from all parts of the world. For these additional features, Dan yr Ogof has been awarded many prestigious awards from the British Tourist Authority, including the honour of receiving three Prince of Wales Awards.

In 1999, following Dan yr Ogof's continuing success as Wales's top tourist attraction, the entire complex received the distinguished title of The National Showcaves Centre for Wales and has been acknowledged as a Site of Special Scientific Interest.

Set amongst the glorious scenery of the Brecon Beacons National Park, at the top of the Swansea Valley, on the A4067 main road to Brecon, the caves lie in an east-west direction and, geologically, are located within the Dinantian limestone of what had been the northern outcrop of the South Wales Coalfield, on the northern slope of the Carmarthen Fan known as the Mynydd Du, or the Black Mountain.

The caves owe their origin partly to the solvent action of water containing carbonic acid filtering through the limestone, and partly to the mechanical action of pebbles, grit and sand which have been swept along by the river.

A visit here is much more than a memorable day out. To step inside the Cathedral cave alone, to marvel at its size and beauty, visitors will find themselves standing inside the largest single chamber to be found in any British showcave.

Cavers come here from all parts of the country, and along with The South Wales Caving Club, they have, through their skill and perseverance, penetrated eleven miles into the mountain to discover a subterranean world of such variety and beauty, that Dan yr Ogof has the added distinction of being the longest and the most impressive cave complex in Europe.

Sadly, this subterranean world of enormous caverns containing spectacular formations, eleven lakes, and waterfalls that reach a hundred feet high, is not accessible to the general public. Until an easier way can be made to reach them, they continue to be the sole province of the experienced caver, but from photographs taken by the intrepid explorers, we are able to appreciate the wonders that exist beyond those lakes discovered in 1912.

It is acknowledged that through man's curiosity is discovery made, and this was certainly the case on a sunny day in June, 1912, when an opening in the rock and the curiosity and courage of two brothers in a coracle brought to light the existence of these caverns which had lain hidden inside the mountain for over 300 million years.

The men were Thomas Ashwell Morgan and his younger brother Jeffrey, who lived at Tŷ Mawr, in the small village of Abercrave, and were the sons of Morgan Morgan who owned two collieries, including one in nearby Ystalyfera. The brothers were later to become owners of their own farms in the area.

Having fished for trout and salmon in the locality, Thomas Ashwell, on seeing the river Llynfell pouring out of its cave at the bottom of a wooded cliff with the same volume and regularity throughout the year, wondered how it had forged its way through the mountain. Curious to investigate, he enlisted the help of his brother Jeffrey and, together, they headed up the valley to Dan yr Ogof Farm, where the river cave was located.

The farm, which was then under the ownership of Mr J. G. Moore Gwyn of Duffryn, Neath, was so named because it was on land immediately below a small cave situated at the top of the cliff. This solitary cave had once been the outlet to the river Llynfell during the Ice Age, but when the retreating ice gouged out a deep valley, the action of shifting rock and earth left the cave high and dry and it is now 140 feet above its original position.

Testing the Coracle at The Pool in 1912
Photo by late Ashwell Morgan. (Reproduced by kind permission of Mr Ashford Price)

After several explorations, we know this dry cave today as Ogof-yr-Esgyrn or Bone Cave.

With the newly created valley, the Llynfell then had to find a new route through the limestone mass and made a new outlet via the present day River Cave.

Wearing only their everyday clothes and carrying a miner's lamp apiece, the Morgan brothers braved the torrent and waded inside the River Cave. At first, the water flowed swiftly about their boots, but about fifty yards inside, they soon found that the water was getting progressively deeper. At this point, too, there was a sudden lowering of the roof which made further exploration on foot quite impossible.

Forced to retreat, they made their way back to the entrance, but ever curious, Jeffrey Morgan noticed an opening high above him on his left. Drawing his brother's attention to it, he climbed up the steep ledge to investigate.

Through the narrow opening, he found that he was looking into what appeared to be another cave. Being of slim build, he hauled himself through and found himself standing in a sand-filled passage with the distant sound of water dripping in the stillness. Excited by his discovery, he shouted for his brother to join him.

Deciding to investigate, they met a solid wall of rock a few yards to their right, but, to their left, the passage meandered into the darkness. Intrigued, they made their way forward. The path, with a headroom of about 12ft, sloped steeply away from them and they instantly noticed the unusual nature of the rock and the marble-like secretions oozing down the walls like miniature waterfalls.

Where the path turned to their right, the roof suddenly lowered and they almost walked into some large formations which hung down like enormous fans. These curious shapes, which curled at the edges, glowed bright orange in their lamps, and when they turned the corner, the brothers could see that they were, in fact, the outer extremities of an enormous sand-coloured flowstone which was curving in a semicircular fashion half way across their path.

About 15ft wide and over 10ft high, this impressive formation appeared to 'pour' out of a deep ledge above them and, impressed, they dubbed it the **Frozen Waterfall.** Excited, the brothers wondered what else there was to find.

Just a few yards ahead they saw a glimmer of water but, to their disappointment, it was a large pool blocking their path. Like the river, it was too deep to cross on foot.

Eager to see what lay beyond, for they were sure they had made a major discovery, the brothers decided they would have to obtain a craft of some sort, to get to the 'other side'. With this in mind, the brothers hurried home, eager to break the news of their discovery to the rest of the family. One can only guess the excitement which generated around the dinner table at **Tŷ Mawr** that night, when they related what they had found, and immediately plans were made for returning to the cave.

This they did the next day, and, with a hastily constructed raft, the brothers, accompanied by their elder brother, Edwin, and their young gamekeeper, Morgan Richard Williams, successfully crossed the pool.

As well as the raft, they took along a good supply of candles to light their way and, curiously, Ashwell wore his service revolver as an extra precaution. They were venturing into unknown territory, and he was not sure what dangers, if any, lay ahead. Once inside the cave, it was quite understandable that they should draw arrows in the sand to help them find their way back to their entry point.

Despite the difficult conditions, with the way often blocked with fallen rock and centuries of accumulated sand deposits, the party made excellent headway deep into the mountain, and although the journey had proved extremely arduous, it had been an exciting and rewarding one. Never had they expected to see so many beautiful creations. Astounded by what they saw, they realised that they had indeed made a major discovery, which was not only unique to the Valley, but to Wales itself.

Once they had crossed the pool, they had seen a stubby white stalactite which clearly resembled a **Parrot** 'clinging' to a ledge on the wall to their left. Below this was another little stalactite, although much squatter. This reminded them of another bird. This twosome drew an amusing little picture, and when, further along, they came across a deep aven just above their heads, with large, almost square shaped boulders jammed together in its roof, and a large cluster of golden-coloured stalactites hanging from a ledge to its left, another picture came to mind, causing the little aven with its cluster of rocks – seemingly looking like bells - to be called **The Belfry,** and the hanging bunch of stalactites **The Bell Ropes.**

Interestingly, the roof of the aven was streaked with a soft, white, spongy substance known as 'moonmilk', and this formed a curious pattern amongst the rocks.

Ahead, the passage dipped and turned. As it did so, the height of the roof varied between six and ten feet. Then, deep crevices formed little grottoes with their own pleasing collection of stalagmites. There were also ledges of jagged rock cutting weird and fanciful shapes, with many of them resembling fierce gargoyles. Just ahead was one which resembled a wolf's head with open jaws. They must have been a strange sight in the black stillness.

The structure of the walls with its dimpling, intrigued them, as did the rippling and circular patterns on many parts of the floor, which had been made by the constant movement of water when the caverns had been flooded. Some parts also resembled a sandy beach after the sea had retreated. Then came a curious find: a continuous spray of water falling in long droplets through tiny holes in the rock, to disappear almost immediately, somewhere in the floor. It was appropriately called **The Showerbath.**

Again, razor sharp rocks cut fanciful and weird shapes in the darkness, then, intriguingly, in one section, the rock took on the appearance of a coral reef with fossils of coral and minute sea shells embedded in the rock. These indicated that the cave had once been at the bottom of a tropical sea, some 315 million years ago.

Next, came stubby little stalactites which were still in the process of

The Bell Ropes
(Reproduced by kind permission of Mr Ashford Price)

growing, and more stalagmite bosses erupting down the walls like miniature waterfalls. This twisting passage then revealed a colony of hollow, pencil-slim stalactites, several inches long, hanging from the roof. Known as straws, they hung in neat geometric rows and provided the brothers with another pleasant encounter.

At the point which we now know as **The Parting of the Ways,** the passage opened out into a wider cavern, and in an oval shaped niche above their heads, they were interested to see a cluster of thin white 'straws' which they thought resembled a **Pin Cushion** and was thus named.

It was probably here, because of the enormous deposits of sand which had accumulated over the centuries and were causing a sizeable obstruction, that they decided to end their first full day's exploration. Even so, they had progressed a staggering 600 feet into the heart of the mountain.

On their third visit to the caves, the party numbered five, when the brothers took along William Lewis, another game keeper. Amongst their equipment was a supply of longer lasting night-lights, to enable them to see more clearly the full beauty of the formations.

Having removed most of the obstacles which had blocked their way the day before, they reached the **Parting of the Ways** with comparative ease, but owing to the enormous sand drifts at The Parting of the Ways, they failed to see the passage which led away to the left.

To them, the way lay straight ahead, and where there are now steps leading upwards, they had to scramble into a crude opening which led them into a narrow u-bend. Having to exercise greater caution in so constricting a place, negotiating the bend was also very time consuming.

Once they had rounded this, their efforts were soon rewarded when they came into full view of a magnificent **Alabaster Pillar** standing under an archway of rock. The sight of this 6ft/1.8m column gleaming white in their lamps caught their breath. It was the most beautiful stalagmite they had yet seen and was made even more spectacular by its clear reflection in the crystal pool surrounding its base.

Beyond, they could see into another section which had even more

The Flitch of Bacon
(Reproduced by kind permission of Mr Ashford Price)

17

Pillar of Salt
(Reproduced by kind permission of Mr Ashford Price)

formations, but they decided that they had gone far enough on that day. Before leaving for the surface, they recorded their visit by pencilling their names on the wall to the left of the Pillar.

During the next visit, another steep climb from the right of the **Pillar** took them into an arched passage only 3ft wide. In the darkness, this passage was made more hazardous by the sharp edges of rock which protruded on either side. Then, after another tight turn with a long climb down to their left, they found they had travelled in a semicircle, were looking at the other side of the **Pillar,** and had come across a perfect example of a 'curtain' formation, about four feet long, with water still dripping down its outer edge. This collected in little pools on the thick stalagmite boss beneath, where circular, lace-like patterns had formed from the constant dripping.

Stained with red-coloured bands produced by iron flowing through the calcite, the curtain looked exactly like slices of bacon. When light shone from behind, it had a translucence that filled them with awe, and it was not surprising that Thomas Ashwell called it **The Flitch of Bacon.**

Where the passage turned again, it took on different characteristics, with the grey rock streaked with what looked like milk spilling down the walls. It also had an impressive array of much larger stalactites, hanging down from a much heightened cavern.

A solitary one, measuring 10ft. long, came to a sharp point and hovered over their heads like an enormous dagger or sword. The dominance of this flat-shaped stalactite was instrumental in them calling this cavern **Dagger Chamber.**

Immediately beneath this impressive stalactite was a three foot high, sand-coloured stalagmite with a curiously scalloped design caused by the continuous splashing of water dripping from the 'dagger'. As this unusually shaped stalagmite tapered towards the top, the beholders thought it had a human form, and since the stalactite above hung over it like the **Sword of Damocles,** they dubbed the curiously shaped formation **Lot's Wife,** or **Pillar of Salt** into which she was eventually turned.

To their surprise, behind the stalactite, and at right angles to the

19

A close up of The Angel
(Reproduced by kind permission of Mr Ashford Price)

Inside Cauldron Chamber: The Curtain
(Reproduced by kind permission of Mr Ashford Price)

passage, lay a grotto-type cavern with an array of slender straws dripping from its roof. On going up the small incline to see where the grotto led, the party was confronted with the amazing sight of a 12ft/3.8m high stalagmite, which gleamed white in their lamps.

Being wider at the bottom, the formation resembled a flowing robe, and when two individual curtain-shaped formations hung from the roof overhead and looked as though they were attached to the top of the pillar like a pair of wings, it looked as though someone had sculptured an angel out of pure marble. The complete effect was breathtaking, and, to the present day visitor, this is probably the best remembered and most popular 'creation' in the entire complex. It is unique. There is no other rock formation to equal it anywhere in Britain.

A few yards ahead, they came across a curious group of five small stalagmites. Nearly 2 feet high, they again tapered towards the top, and looked like hooded figures with bowed heads and, having caught the imagination of the explorers, they were inevitably called **The Nuns.**

Next to this amusing little group was another entertaining feature, in the shape of a much squatter stalagmite with a form that resembled a chicken sitting on its nest, and this was appropriately called **The Broody Hen.**

Immediately above the **Nuns** were several pointed stalactites. Grouped together, they hung down like a ragged curtain and formed a stunning display, as did the nearby 4ft long stalactite boss, flowing down a niche in long ringlets. In the light they also shone like white marble.

Inspired by this section, which had proved to be the most beautiful, the brothers forged ahead, clearing the way as they went, before climbing up into another narrow passageway where the roof curved like a nave. In the distance they heard the sound of rushing water. They hastened on. The passage fell sharply again to the left and brought them to a section where the roof was considerably higher. At the bottom of the slope they were faced with more marble-like stalagmites hanging over the ledge like icicles. Beneath, a deep cavern, whose ceiling was nearly 4ft high, extended across to reach the footway we now know as Western Passage. The floor of this cavern was littered with boulders, amongst which were pools of clear water that reflected the surrounding rocks. To the right of this was yet another opening, through which the sound of cascading water grew louder.

After another difficult climb, now made easy by a flight of steps, the party found themselves inside an enormous cavern some 40ft/13m high, with grey craggy walls which were again streaked with white. It was the largest they had encountered, and, surprisingly, the air felt extremely fresh for a place which was 590ft/180m underground.

The floor revealed an assortment of stalagmites, but it was the sight of an 18ft/5.5m long 'curtain' hanging from the ceiling that brought forth gasps of admiration. Like the Flitch of Bacon, traces of iron had stained the calcite with red strips. This, with the addition of folding caused by strong draughts, gave this amazing structure the realistic look of material. As the cavern's most outstanding feature, it has the distinction of being the longest free-hanging curtain in Britain. Whether the explorers could see its beauty in the light of their flickering candles, we cannot say, but they called this impressive cave **Cauldron Chamber.**

The water they had heard gushing in the distance came from a small waterfall, pouring out of a deep hollow on the far side of the cavern to form a running stream. Next, they found themselves in a sand filled cavern with a much lower roof. A few steps inside, they came to the edge of a precipitous slope, but the most incredible sight was that of an enormous slab of flat rock forming a bridge over the dark, empty void. The walls and roof of the cavern were almost black and gave the place a forbidding and eerie atmosphere. On the other side of the wall they could hear the sound of water and realised they were standing just above the river.

Not knowing how safe the rocks were, they descended the slope and found yet another opening, leading to a tunnel. Going through, the roof decreased considerably, and at its end, they found a small lake, about 12 yards long, stretching into the darkness. Despite coming up against an obstacle of this nature, they still wished to continue with the exploration. For them, the adventure was not yet over, and if they were to see what lay beyond the

The Extent of the 1966 Exploration

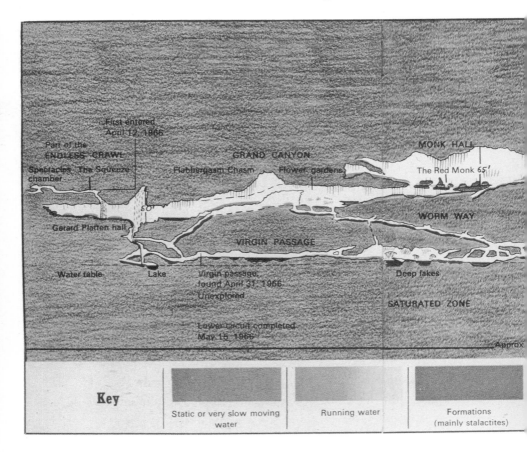

First entered
April 12, 1966

Part of the
ENDLESS CRAWL

GRAND CANYON

MONK HALL

Spectacles The Squeeze
chamber

Flabbergasm Chasm   Flower gardens

The Red Monk 65'

Gerard Platten hall

SO!

WORM WAY

VIRGIN PASSAGE

Water table   Lake   Virgin passage,
found April 31, 1966.
Unexplored

Deep lakes

SATURATED ZONE

Lower circuit completed
May 15, 1966

Approx

Key

Static or very slow moving
water

Running water

Formations
(mainly stalactites)

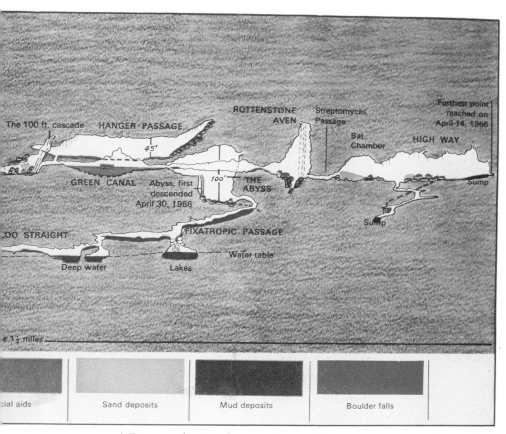

A Diagram showing the main feature of the new cave system discovered at Dan yr Ogof in 1966, published in the Observer *magazine*

25

lake, then something more dependable than a raft was required. Certainly, their determination to continue far outweighed the difficulty of getting a craft through the opening above the river, let alone down the slope leading into the tunnel, and it was with this determination that they set off for home.

The only craft they considered suitable for crossing the lake was a coracle, and on their way to the entrance, they found an alternative route which did not entail making any difficult climbs and would make the return journey much easier. Before leaving, however, the party again recorded their visit, by inserting their names inside a glass bottle and leaving it, along with a Thermos flask and one of the stubby candles on a shelf close to the **Alabaster Pillar.** On the wall behind the objects, someone scratched the date '1912'.

The next day, the brothers caught a train from Abercrave station to Carmarthen, where they got a coracle from a reputed maker and then took it home on the train. Made of ash wood and willow, and covered in calico before being waterproofed with tar, coracles weigh between 30–40 lbs. and are usually carried strapped across a man's shoulder. This was probably the way it was carried to the lake, rather than being dragged through the difficult passages.

Before entrusting the craft on to the lake, though, they first tested it on the pool they had first crossed. Unlike a rowing boat, a coracle requires a different technique to manoeuvre. Its rounded structure enables it to rotate in any direction. To get it to travel in one direction, however, requires a different strategy, especially with only a single paddle to move it along. This event was recorded on camera, and the now familiar photograph taken at the pool shows Thomas Ashwell sitting inside the coracle.

It was Ashwell Morgan who decided to cross the lake with one end of a rope tied to the coracle and the other held by his brother Jeffrey, who later wrote: 'Placed on the lake, it appeared a frail craft to be entrusted with the mission of carrying a human being into the Stygian darkness into which the lake disappeared," but it was into that darkness, along a narrow channel, that Ashwell Morgan manoeuvred the coracle, with a tumultuous roar of cascading water sounding somewhere in the distance.

On the other side of the lake, Ashwell found himself on a sandy beach and summoned Jeffrey to join him. Then, after going along what seemed to be a long passage with a higher roof, they came across another stretch of water. With Jeffrey holding on to the rope, this, too, Ashwell navigated, until, to his great surprise, he came across a third lake, where the sound of water was greatly amplified in the enclosed space. This made Ashwell suspect that he was heading towards a powerful waterfall.

Not being able to see from where the water was coming, he wondered whether it was pouring into the lake, or leaving it as a torrent. Afraid that the coracle was in danger of being swamped, or even swept away to unknown depths, he gave the signal to return.

Beforehand, the brothers had arranged a series of whistles to communicate with one another, and when Ashwell gave the approved whistle to be pulled back, the roar of the torrent made it difficult for Jeffrey to hear. Not being able to see his brother in the darkness, or the circumstances in which he found himself, Jeffrey had some worrying moments in deciding what his brother wanted but, rather than risk leaving him to the mercy of the water, he pulled him back to safety.

Afterwards, it was revealed that neither of them could remember what method of communication they eventually used, as during those worrying moments, both men had forgotten what had actually transpired. One can only presume that the final instruction had been a very loud one.

With having to abandon all hope of crossing the lakes, the brothers made one final visit to the caves alone, and since their family had expressed some concern for their safety, they left instructions that if they had not emerged by 4 o'clock, then a search party was to be organised. Still looking for new passages, they noticed a narrow opening they had not seen before, and, ever curious, they decided to investigate. Jeffrey was again the one to be lowered into the darkness, and as he made his way along the twisting passage, he found it more intimidating than any of the others when jagged pieces of rock protruded dangerously in his path.

When, at last, he came across the **Alabaster Pillar** on his left, he realised that he had found yet another way out. Excitedly, he hurried back to inform his brother. They used this passage to return to the surface, and when, eventually, they could see the glow from the half-burned candles which they had placed at The Parting of the Ways, they realised that the passage they were in had led off it and had gone unnoticed when they had passed through earlier. Now known as Western Passage, this is the route by which present day visitors make their way back from Bridge Chamber, thus completing, as the Morgans had, a circular route back to the entrance.

Satisfied that they had explored all the passages known to them, the two brothers made for the entrance, collecting, as they went, all the half-burned candles. By the time they had reached what was thought to be their entry point, the candles had burnt dangerously low and, with the flickering light casting deceiving shadows on the walls, the brothers had great difficulty in finding the narrow opening through which they had come. They had some worrying moments as they went on searching, and with the last of the candles almost burnt out, they finally succeeded in locating the elusive opening just before the four o'clock deadline.

It had been a great disappointment to them that they could not share with the people of the Valley the marvels they had seen. Until an easier way could be found to enter the caves, they would have to remain as inaccessible as ever. News of the discovery though, spread down the Valley and beyond, and the brothers were hailed as heroes.

During those incredible days, the brothers had shown great courage in venturing into unknown territory. Without their curiosity and perseverance, we might never have known that such a magical world existed. And whilst Ashwell and Jeffrey Morgan had come through their endeavours without serious incident, they had shared many anxious moments. For, knowing how isolated they were, they had not been in a position to summon help had one of them suffered an accident. But in spite of the risks taken, they had come through their experiences unscathed.

Such an important discovery was, however, something to be

celebrated, and sightseers soon made their way to the site in a variety of ways, arriving on foot, horseback, bicycle, and pony and trap. Many ventured up the cascades and into the river-cave itself, but this was soon discouraged when it was found that even young children were trying to emulate the explorers by venturing into the river cave and climbing up the ledge; a venture that was considered too dangerous. This was, therefore, prohibited when the owner put up a 'No Trespass' notice.

It was the Morgan family's dream to open the caves to the general public. The caves had great potential as a tourist attraction and promised to be successful, but before they could do so, they would have to negotiate for the purchase of the farm and its land.

In two years' time the world was at war and, for the time being, the caves reverted back to the hidden world they had once been. It was not until 1939 that their beauty was finally revealed to the general public.

With regard to the solitary cave high up in the cliff known as Yr Ogof, the discovery of the caves had naturally brought a resurgence of interest in this remote cavern which, for centuries, had remained unexplored because it had been considered too dangerous to enter. Being so, successive landowners had barred entry by blocking up its entrance with a wall and a padlocked gate.

Suddenly, with the discovery of the lower caves, the cave became the subject of great speculation when many wondered if it, too, contained beautiful formations, but the Valley had to wait another eleven years before that particular question was answered. When Yr Ogof was eventually explored in 1923, its secrets began to be revealed in the most dramatic way, and continued to do so for the next forty years, surprising us all with some amazing finds.

Bone Cave:
1923 Exploration

With life returning to some kind of normality after the end of the Great War and interest in the caves extending beyond Wales, there was a significant step forward when the first geological survey was carried out, in 1922, by R. E. M. Evans, BSc., FGS. of the Crumlin School of Mines.

During his visit, Mr Evans produced sectional drawings showing, in particular, the position of 'Yr Ogof' when it served as a drainage channel for the river Llynfell during the Ice Age, and again after the cave had been lifted 140 feet above the floor of the valley, an action which left the river to find a fresh outlet through the limestone mass, until it finally emerged through a new opening which we now know as the River Cave.

In cutting their way through the mountain, the undermining action of the subterranean streams was instrumental in causing a large slice of the cliff face to collapse. We can see where it broke away as we climb up the gorge to the Bone Cave. It is interesting to note that the waterfall from Castell-y-Geifr (Goats' Castle), above the cave, pours directly into Pwll-y-Wydden (Swallow's Hole), to feed the underground channels leading down to the River Cave, and that a large number of galleries which branch from them serve as outlets for the main caves during the rainy season.

During March and July of 1923, the caves were partially explored by the newly formed Archaeological Society of the then University of Wales and Monmouthshire in conjunction with the National Museum of Wales in Cardiff. At the exploration was Dr Mortimer Wheeler, who had excavated many Roman Forts in Wales, including Y Gaer, near Brecon. He went on to become the country's most eminent archaeologist and was knighted for his services in 1975.

As Keeper of the Museum's Archaeological Department, which he had set up in 1920, Mortimer Wheeler arrived at Dan yr Ogof Farm and set up camp there with a party of students from the University where he also lectured. Joining him was fellow archaeologist, Mr R. H. D'Elboux, from Gravesend, Kent, who directed the excavations.

Then, under the hospitality of Mr Jones, the farm's tenant, who had given "untiring courtesy" throughout their stay, the party entered the main caves, but they, too, found that the lakes were still "an insurmountable obstacle". It was their visit to the solitary cave which had made their venture worthwhile. To reach the mouth of the cave, which faces north-east, the party had to negotiate the very steep slope which was no more than a sheep track and covered with scree. At the top it turned sharply to the left. Within two yards of the entrance, they found that the ground sloped precipitously away from them, with very little surface earth covering the rock. Of the wall built across the entrance, only 1½ft remained to the right of the padlocked gate. In all, the entrance, including the wall, measured 8ft. 8 ins across and was only 4ft. 9 ins high.

Within a few yards of them entering, the height of the passage lessened considerably and their way was blocked by a large roof-fall. Once through, they found that the passage was 22ft long and took them in a north-to-south direction until it eventually widened into a single large chamber. Relieved that they had finally reached the centre of the cave, the party were even more relieved to stand upright once more, for although the width of the passage had varied between 8ft and 15ft where it met the chamber, the ceiling had, for the greater part, remained an uncomfortable 4ft high.

After entering, they noticed that the interior was sloping to the right, with a flat roof measuring from 14-15½ feet high. The scene which confronted them was one of complete chaos, with the greater part of the

Tableau of domestic life in Bone Cave

floor strewn with assorted debris and boulders of various dimensions which had fallen from the roof. The centre of the floor was also wet from roof drippings which would account for the size of the two stalagmite bosses and explain why the large boulders had bonded securely to them.

A thick layer of stalagmite also covered its walls, with a steep flow against the eastern one. To the right of the bosses was a curious semicircle of stones about 4ft high. It looked like a miniature Stonehenge, and gave the chamber an instant air of mystery.

The flatness of the roof was due to the horizontal nature of the rock, and because of the constant dripping of water, it had ultimately become streaked with the creamy-coloured substance known as 'moonmilk'. In places, it hung in thick, spongy clumps and had traces of copper-coloured segments which glinted in the light.

Contributing to the chaos was an enormous strip of rock which had not entirely broken free of the roof. It had remained in an upright position after its fall, and where it had pierced the floor, it, too, had become embedded in the stalagmite boss.

In the difficult conditions, measurements taken indicated that the chamber was 58½ft wide, east to west, and that it had a depth of 36ft north to south. Where possible, inspection of the floor revealed dark brown, calcareous loam, or cave-earth, which was similar to that found in other dry caves in Britain. It varied in thickness from 1 inch to 2 feet in the deeper pockets, and where it had come into contact with water, it was extremely muddy. There were also deposits of fine sand and gravel which had come mainly from the millstone outcrop of Castell-y-Geifr above.

Along the western half of the northern wall there was an even deeper pocket of sand which had come from a small passage in the N/E corner. It was the driest part of the chamber. They also discovered a small passage at the back of the cave which was studded with stalagmites. It provided a channel for a small stream which entered the cave during wet weather, before disappearing amongst the boulders.

Cave deposits often provide vital information about how our predecessors lived in earliest times, but from the haphazard nature of the interior, the archaeologists faced a difficult task to prove that the cave had once been inhabited. Out of an estimated area of 230 sq. yards, only 60 could be effectively excavated.

From previous evidence, it is known that cave dwellers usually built their fires just inside the entrance of a cave, and on the premise that there was a hearth there, a trial pit was dug. However, after striking rock at a depth of 2 feet, the only objects they could find were a few animal bones and, strangely, an iron staple and bar, which had probably come from the iron gate at the entrance. The soil was then replaced. A few yards ahead, where the cave widened, a second pit was chosen. Here, the upper surface consisted of fine, reddish brown earth, in which was a large amount of rabbit droppings. A section measuring some 10½ square feet was levelled to a depth of 7 inches. Below this there was a 3-5 inch layer of clay-like earth which hardened when it came into contact with the air. Penetrating it were several boulders.

In spite of this, the party made their first exciting discovery, when a bone pin was found. Measuring 4 inches long, it had a trellis pattern around the head. It was, though, minus its point. This little item from the Bronze Age spurred the archaeologists on, and when they came across a layer of burnt hearth material some 20 inches from the surface, they knew they had found evidence of human habitation. Measuring some 36 inches square, the layer varied in thickness according to the boulders in which it was scattered. Where the boulders allowed, the whole area was excavated to a depth of 5 feet. Careful examination revealed some significant finds which, to their surprise, included some charred human remains.

Among the items found were:

(1) The upper half of another bone pin, again, with the same distinctive pattern around its head.

(2) A finger-ring consisting of two strands of twisted silver with a 'rope' pattern, terminating in a bezel and flanked by four globules.

Unfortunately, half the bezel was missing and the circlet was distorted by damage.

Rings with globules go back to the mid second century, when they were much smaller, but similarities with this particular type suggested a fourth-century date, during the Roman occupation of Wales.

(3) A brass replica of a Roman, Constantine I coin. (AD 330-340) also surfaced. These brass replicas were used when the original coins were in short supply. It was the practice for brass copies to be made locally and circulated as legal tender.

(4) A grey coloured tessera – a small cubic stone used in Roman mosaics. This was a curious find, since no mosaics had been found in the area.

A selection of domestic objects was also found, at depths ranging from 10-18 inches from the surface. These included:

Shards of Early Bronze Age pottery:

(1) A piece of hand-made, coarse sandy-brown ware with a deeply incised trellis pattern, which had come from a jar.

(2) A grey, fine-gritted ware with a buff outer surface, likely to be part of the deep collar of a fine overhanging rim urn, also with an incised lattice pattern.

Hand-made jars were usually well fired but coarse and were bucket- or barrel-shaped, with finger-printed lugs for handles. The diagonal trellis design incised around the necks is indicative of the Early Bronze Age and is distinct from those used during the Middle Bronze Age, with its tradition of fluted decoration.

Other fragments of pottery shards were identified by Mortimer Wheeler as having been of Romano/British origin. They included:

(1) Several pieces from Ollas, often called 'Rotten Pots". These were used for mixed dishes such as stews. Rims from three of these vessels were found. One rim was similar in form to that excavated at Corbridge, in 1911, alongside a cache of Roman coins from the Vespasian period (AD 155). This particular piece was thought to came from a pot belonging to the first

half of the second century AD.

(2) The second rim was dated to the Antonine period in the second to the third century, and the largest piece was ascribed to the fourth century AD.

(3) Fragments of a light grey jar with a trellis pattern which came from the same vessel, was dated AD 50-125.

This productive hearth also produced several fragments from various Cavetto (almost square-shaped) cooking pots from the 2nd to 4th Century. (AD 280-350 and AD 200-370). There were also some thin strips of bronze wire. One piece had been pierced at the top and near the base, and was probably a clasp. A semicircle of iron also surfaced. It had corroded and was probably a handle. There were also three tiny fragments of fire-polished glass, which could have come from a colourless, blown vessel, probably a beaker.

Another tiny fragment of glass was recognised as having been part of a flaring rim of another colourless, blown beaker. Expert examination showed that it had been wheel-polished. It is noted that glass pre-dating the Roman occupation has not been found anywhere in Britain.

Just 4 yards away, another area of burnt wood and ashes was found, but as the hearths were separated by a mere 2 inches of unburnt earth, this clearly indicated that they belonged to two different periods. Among the ashes was a ring made from a strip of coiled bronze, twisted into a triple spiral. Basically of British origin, examples of these rings have been found in various interments, ranging from the Bronze Age to Saxon times. As this ring was comparable with those found at Glastonbury, in Wiltshire, and Maiden Castle, in Dorset, it was ascribed to the Antonine period of the 4th century.

It was between the two hearths that the human bones were found. They had been scattered, probably as the result of rabbits scratching around for food, or by rock movements caused by water sweeping through the cave. They had been mixed with animal bones, and some had been blackened from being in contact with the fires. A complete jaw bone was found wedged between the boulders. It had been pierced by a rock. Curiously, it was resting against a sheep's jaw bone. Two halves of a human skull, which had been separated after being pierced by falling rock, were found several feet apart.

Moving deeper into the chamber, the group discovered another hearth layer within the circle of fallen rocks, which had an entrance of just 2 feet wide. Inside, scattered amongst the smaller boulders, were charcoal and other charred human bones. The layer also produced pottery fragments, two undecorated bone pins and, curiously, an indeterminate scrap of bronze.

Among the fragments of pottery were:

(1) The rim of a black bowl.

(2) The rim of a small olla or beaker made of black ware which was dated to the late first or early second century.

(3) The rim of a black olla with an overhanging rim. It was similar in design to the one found in the first hearth and dated to the fourth-century AD.

No items of pottery were found to be in contact with the remains to suggest that they had been buried with the dead, but there were shards close by and at the same level, which included a piece of thick, coarse red ware, of Romano/British origin, with a criss-cross design. This was believed to be a local imitation of the smooth, black pottery in use at that time.

A piece of grey Bronze Age pottery was found close to a skull fragment. A part of a human skull was also found in sand 6 inches from the surface. A surprising find was a nail, 4 inches long.

It was evident from the amount of charcoal and pottery found in the hearth layers, that the cave had been occupied at its earliest during the period known as Middle Bronze Age III – (1050-850 BC), and on two separate occasions sometime during the Roman occupation in the second and fourth centuries, AD.

From the accumulation of boulders in one part of the cave, it was assumed that the last occupants must have done some clearing from time to time to create flat surfaces for their comfort.

The animal bones consisted mainly of sheep or lamb, but there were those of pigs and oxen. Many had been cut by a sharp instrument for use as ornamental clips, and one ox bone had been split, presumably to get to the marrow, which would have been considered a delicacy.

The human bones were carefully assembled and taken away for examination by Dr C. W. Edwards from the Natural History Department of the British Museum, and Professor Sir Arthur Keith of the Royal College of Surgeons. From the evidence presented, the bones belonged to two adult men, a woman and a young child, with fragments belonging to one or two more individuals.

Examination of the leg bones revealed that the individuals had been in the habit of sitting in a squatting position. There was also evidence of osteo-arthritis and that the child had suffered from rickets. In his comments, Sir Keith said, that from their condition and from the soil clinging to them, the bones could not have been more than medieval in date. From the animal bones and pottery shards found in the cave, it can be believed that our dwellers ate well and that the Bronze Age family had even applied their skills to carving pins out of animal bone.

There is evidence that a village existed in the area during prehistoric times. Taking into account that there was plenty of head room in the cave, it made an ideal dwelling place and gave protection from the elements. It also overlooked a fertile valley which had an abundance of water. Cave entrances were often vulnerable to attack, but as this one had a long passage, any dweller living here would have felt safe. Its remoteness, too, would have given extra protection.

The exploration of Yr Ogof, though, was far from over. Owing to the haphazard nature of the interior and the thickness of the stalagmite bosses, which made clearing away the fallen rock difficult, it was not possible to continue at that time, but already a wealth of information and bounty had emerged to justify keeping the archaeologists interested. It was felt that Yr Ogof had still many more of its secrets to reveal.

Following the success of the exploration, details of the artefacts were reported in the 1924 edition of *The Archaeologia Cambrensis* by Mr R. H. D'Elboux.

Main Caves: 1937 Exploration

1937 proved a significant year in the continuing exploration of Dan yr Ogof. With interest in the caves now established, a party of speleologists arrived early in the year to carry out a survey. Focusing their attention on Cauldron Chamber, they were surprised to discover that there was another cavern immediately above.

Using fixed ladders, they found themselves climbing into an enormous chamber which contained a spectacular display of red-coloured stalagmites. A stream was also seen flowing out of the chamber to descend into The Cauldron below. **Red Chamber** is stated as being large enough to hold 200 people.

During the summer, an attempt was made to explore the caves beyond the third lake. This was initiated by Mr Gerard Platten of the Mendip Exploration Society which already had a number of explorations to its credit. He first heard about the 1912 discovery from an enthusiastic and experienced pot-holer, Ernest Roberts, from Yorkshire, who had been on a walking holiday in the area the previous September, and had learned of the caves after meeting Jeffrey Morgan at *The Gwyn Arms*, a popular inn and a short distance from Dan yr Ogof.

Having received permission to enter the caves from Mr Eliphaz Morgan, the eldest of the Morgan brothers, who was now the official owner, Messrs Platten and Roberts arrived at Dan yr Ogof in May with a team of expert cavers from their respective areas.

They came equipped with ladders, acetylene lamps, and inflatable rubber dinghies, each one weighing about 7 pounds and described by Roberts as 'a cross between a baby's bath and a balloon tyre.' They recorded that, on reaching the First Lake, they found 'it was some 12 yards/10.8m long and very deep.' Like Ashwell and Jeffrey Morgan, they, too, could hear 'a great thunder of water.' On the other side, there was a steep sand bank which separated it from the Second Lake. This was described as 'a shallow pool, some 20 yards long, and was easy to cross.'

Beyond this, they found themselves standing on a narrow, sandy beach and were surprised to see the extent of the Third Lake which 'simply ran into the distance.' The water was deep and they required the use of a dinghy. Once across, they found that the roar of water came not from a powerful waterfall, as was first thought in 1912, but from a series of small but swiftly flowing cataracts.

The river was in flood at the time, and as it affected the underground system of Dan yr Ogof, the party encountered an extremely strong current on the lake which proved too troublesome for their boats. They abandoned the mission and tried to cross the cataracts some other way.

On returning to the surface, the explorers had to agree that they had been surprised by the size of the lakes. They had been much larger than expected, and taking into account the difficulties involved, they had to agree that the crossing made by Jeffrey and Ashwell Morgan with a coracle had been 'a great effort'.

Encouraged to know that the Third Lake had at last been crossed, Thomas Ashwell was anxious to participate, and in company with his nephew, Mr Ashford Price (and Uncle of the present owner), and a friend, Miss Coote, who was also a member of the exploration party, they returned to the caves in August with the object of going beyond the cataracts. Knowing that the third lake was less of a threat, they took along a two-man boat made of wood and canvas. After securing the craft, the trio climbed up the side of the first cataract and found themselves wading in deep water for a distance of 50 yards/45.7m. Then, to their surprise, under a very low roof, they found a fourth lake at the top of the second cataract, which again 'seemed to stretch far into the distance'.

There was a strong current here, too, and not being able to cross at that particular time, they returned to their boat. Miss Coote, though, daring the cold water, swam all the way back.

A month later, and still in poor weather, Gerard Platten and Ernest Roberts brought along a team totalling seventeen men, and, after two unsuccessful attempts due to the extreme conditions, a force of ten men finally crossed the Fourth Lake on Sunday, 20th September. It was described as being 'a backwater with no visible signs of an inlet'. They also noticed that the area was covered with a frothy layer of peat-like deposits that had been washed down from the surface and which occur after every flood.

On the second attempt to go beyond the fourth lake, Miss Coote noticed a long passage, with a strip of land about 15 yards long which made a useful 'landing stage'.

In crossing the lake, however, they had to avoid colliding with a large formation which hung low over the water like an enormous curtain. They also had to avoid jagged pieces of rock which suddenly loomed precariously out of the darkness.

Firmly convinced that the fourth lake held the key to further discoveries, one caver, on carrying out a survey, fell in when his boat accidentally overturned, and finding himself in the deepest part, discovered that water entered the lake via a submerged channel on the far side. He also found that the lake could be waded across if care were exercised to escape the deep channel which crossed it diagonally from left to right. To minimise this threat and to make further exploration possible, he suggested that the lake should be lowered sufficiently to reveal the hidden entrance to the channel. The only practical way of achieving this was to blast a deep notch in the rock shelf. Permission to do this was obtained and, following the blast, the lake was lowered sufficiently to reveal the submerged entrance lying just 6 inches below the surface.

Beyond the lake, a short climb led to another passage which took them into an enormous chamber, some sixty feet high. At the far end, enormous boulders created an almost insurmountable wall of rock. Convinced that there were other passages beyond the obstruction, the party began the strenuous task of removing the rocks from the cave they called **Boulder Chamber,** and found that their efforts soon led to new finds. Among the party was Mr Ashwell Morgan, who was ever eager to make new discoveries and took along a field telephone – one of the first links the explorers had with the surface.

Whilst in **Boulder Chamber,** a large aven was found, for which Ashwell Morgan built a special three-staged ladder to enable them to climb the initial 25ft approach. At the top of the aven, a strong draught gave every indication that there were other passages beyond, but on investigation, they were not considered to be extensive. Another large aven was also discovered beyond the Fourth Lake. When explored, the cavers found, to their surprise, a passageway which led them back towards the Show-cave's entrance.

On the 30th September, Gerard Platten organised a further trip, and returned again in October and November when spectacular finds were made. During the October visit, the party, who had styled themselves **The Dragon Group,** discovered a cavern displaying a spectacular array of straw stalactites measuring 7ft in length. It was named **Ashwell Morgan's Palace, or Straw Chamber.** An impressive cavern, named **Wigmore Hall,** was another major find and was the longest in that section. Also, they came across another well-decorated cave they called **Corbell's Chamber,** with an enormous pile of rocks in its centre. Beyond was a much lower passage, the entrance to which was marked by a thick band of white 'straws' stretching from wall to wall.

In November, Gerard Platten's group advanced a further 100 yards and found more caverns in which they could hear the sound of water somewhere in the distance, but they soon suffered a setback when they encountered what was described as a 'particularly filthy way', called the **Mud Crawl.** Despite a strong draught blowing through, the party found their way blocked by 'a terrible squeeze' at the top of an opening 5 feet high. Having crawled in thick mud, a member described the squeeze as 'a drain pipe half filled with water'. Undeterred by the temporary halt to their explorations, Gerrard Platten made one final attempt to go further, but had to agree that the conditions of the **Mud Crawl** made further progress almost impossible.

The side passages leading to the Crawl were all explored but only one member, P. Backhouse, managed to get a little further, to add another 60 yards to Dan yr Ogof's total length. In all, the efforts of **The Dragon Group** had succeeded in doubling the length of that discovered in 1912.

Forever interested in the progress of the exploration, the Morgan Brothers met members of the **Dragon Group** at *The Gwyn Arms,* to be told, that until the narrow passage could be passed, no further exploration of Dan yr Ogof was possible. There was, however, one encouraging ray of hope, the strong draught felt blowing down this narrow tube gave the group every indication that there were other passages beyond, and all waiting to be explored.

At this time, the Morgan brothers were planning to get the main caves open to the public and formed a company called The Dan yr Ogof Swansea Valley Caves Limited.

In preparing the site, the old farmhouse was demolished to make way for Tea Rooms, and the momentous task of making an entrance to link up with the explored passages was undertaken by a team of twenty-two men recruited from the locality who drilled into the rock face. Small explosive charges were also used to force a way through.

With power provided by a turbine driven by the cascades tumbling out of the River Cave, electricity was supplied to the caves and rails were laid into the man-made tunnel on which wagons could roll to take out the debris and the newly excavated material. They also removed 400 tons of sand which had accumulated after the flood waters of centuries had receded.

A bridge was then built across the pool on which the Morgan brothers had first tested their coracle, now named the **Coracle Pool,** and concrete paths and flights of steps were made without spoiling the natural look of the caves. There followed the great undertaking of providing the right kind of lighting to 'show off' the formations to their best advantage.

The long awaited opening to the public came on August Bank Holiday, 1939, and was an instant success. It was reported that 5,000 visitors came during the first week, with 1,000 visiting on the Bank Holiday Monday itself, and 600 and 700 respectively during the following Tuesday and Wednesday. In total, 200,000 visitors came to the caves in the short time they were open. It was an unforgettable experience for many, myself included. As we can see, the lighting has been done with brilliant effect, enabling us all to enjoy the spectacle of so many beautiful creations in their own unique settings.

During the first few years, visitors were taken around in groups by well informed guides, but nowadays, with the advent of such technology as piped music and taped commentaries, visitors can amble through the caverns at their leisure to enjoy the unusual atmosphere of the various sections which are enhanced by the addition of carefully selected music.

This is clearly evident in **Cauldon Chamber,** where today's visitors can see **The Curtain** displayed to its best advantage by the very effective lighting arrangement. This also highlights various interesting features in the roof. On looking up, one can see the distinct difference in the colour of the rock which indicates that originally there were two caves before earth tremors in ancient times caused the floor of the uppermost one to collapse. This would account for the enormous pile of boulders which the brothers had found strewn across the floor.

The circular holes in the roof would also have intrigued the explorers. These had been caused by the continuous swirling of water cutting through the rock for thousands of years, when there had been a water-filled cave above.

During that summer of 1939, shortly after the opening, the daughters of Mr Ashwell Morgan acquired an inflatable boat and bravely set off to cross the lakes themselves. Wearing nothing more waterproof than a pair of wellington boots over their riding britches, the Misses Gwenie and Brenda Morgan got as far as the third lake and found it an exciting experience. At the time, such a crossing made by novices was considered a daring achievement, and one which Miss Brenda Morgan recalled many years later, with pride.

Owing to the success of the caves, and the interest they had generated over the past two years, the recognition of South Wales as an important caving area came when members of the British Speleological Association held its fourth Annual Conference in Swansea, in August that year. Following a visit to the caves, it was the opinion of many of the eminent speleologists present that Dan yr Ogof contained some of the finest examples of stalactite and stalagmite formations in the country. This accolade, coming so early in Dan yr Ogof's history, greatly boosted its prestige as a tourist attraction. The Mendip Exploration Society also added their own 'stamp' of recognition when, at their Annual General Meeting, held in *The Gwyn Arms*, they appointed Mr Edwin Morgan as Vice President of the Society.

In addition, the caves attracted the attention of caving enthusiasts from all over the country, and a Welsh branch of the Mendip Exploration Society was formed. Unfortunately, these activities were carried out during a time of great instability, when war was imminent, and when war was declared on 3rd September, 1939, the caves were forced to close and were commandeered by the War Department for storing explosives and ammunition, with Mr Gerard Platten providing expert advice.

Following the acquisition, the newly made entrance was sealed off with a steel-shuttered door and the approach was cordoned off with barbed wire. Even the owners were forbidden from entering the caves. The explosives arrived by train at Ystradgynlais railway station, situated down the valley, and were driven in lorries to Dan yr Ogof. The storage of such militarily sensitive material was kept a closely guarded secret, and the question as to what was being stored in the caves became the subject of great speculation for many years.

Even at the end of the war, entry into the caves was delayed when the Military failed to hand them back to the family, This, of course, caused great frustration when it was the family's intention to reopen them without further delay. It was also unfortunate that the sad demise of Mr Eliphaz Morgan had delayed the reopening of the caves. As the senior brother, he had willed the property to his four brothers, Thomas Ashwell, Jeffrey, William Edwin and Captain Howell Morgan. Sadly, during this time, Mr Jeffrey Morgan had also died, which meant that the settlement of the estate took longer to resolve. Only when this had been achieved, could plans go ahead to re-open the caves.

It transpired that, during the 'occupation', some accidental damage had occurred to some of the delicate formations, which included the Parrot losing its tail and The Sword of Damocles its tip.

Once again, workmen began the awesome task of removing the 300 – 400 tons of sand which had accumulated over the years. A special covered way leading to the entrance was also constructed to protect the visitor from the risk of stones falling from the overhead cliff. As an extra precaution, a protective covering of wire mesh was also put in place along the sides of the cliff. The Tea Rooms were repainted and refurbished, and when all work had been completed, the caves were re-opened to the public in August, 1964.

While people began flocking back to the Show-cave in record numbers, further explorations were taking place in the rest of the complex to add yet another successful chapter to the history of Dan yr Ogof.

Bone Cave: 1938 Exploration

1938 was a momentous year in the continuing story of the little cave known as Yr Ogof, when significant finds of great historic value were found. Following the success of the Mendip Exploration Society in the main caves, a fellow member, Mr Edmund J Mason, who was also one of the country's top archaeologists, was given permission in March to continue with the excavation of Yr Ogof.

Again, under the directorship of Sir Cyril Fox, the National Museum of Wales expressed their interest and sent along their representative, Mr W.F. Grimes (later Professor), Chief Assistant at the Department of Archaeology. Assisting in the excavations was the late Dr H. N. Savory, another eminent archaeologist and Keeper of Archaeology at the National Museum. Included in the party was Mrs Audrey Williams, curator of the archaeological items at the Swansea Museum. She was later to became the wife of Mr Mason.

Exploration started in June, and the first task was to explore the small passage which the 1923 expedition had discovered in the north-east corner of the chamber. This was found to be studded with small stalagmites and led upwards at a very steep angle to a small cave which ended at the top of the cliff. Due to its steepness, it was very difficult to explore and considered unlikely to have been inhabited; because of its close proximity to the surface, it also served as a channel for the small stream which entered the cave in wet weather but which disappeared down a single hole among the boulders, probably to join the lower levels of the cave complex.

On the opposite side of the chamber there was another small opening, about a foot high. This was also too small to explore. As the accumulation of boulders covering the floor presented a problem, these had to be cleared before excavation could start. To this end, the party enlisted the help of the South Wales members of the Society, who were only too happy to lend muscle and expertise to this important project. Where boulders had adhered to the stalagmite boss, they had to be laboriously broken up with sledge hammer and pick-axe.

During this process, the party were amazed to see the thickness of the two stalagmite bosses which had fused into one enormous mass. The large slice of rock, which had fallen from the roof and become embedded in the boss, proved difficult to remove, and the archaeologists had to resort to using a small but controlled charge of dynamite to clear the area.

During the removal of the rubble, some more human finds were made in a pocket of sand close to the north wall. These included a femora, vertebrae, ribs and a mandible. Then, pending clearance of the floor, a white cross was painted on the wall to mark the spot. When this work had been completed, three days later, the floor was divided into square yards and each area given a letter of the alphabet for identification purposes. Marked in white paint on the walls, capital letters were used down the length of the cave whilst the smaller letters were painted across its width.

The system was to excavate each square individually, with all material from the area passed through a sieve to ensure that nothing was lost. It was then labelled with the square in which it was found, but their working area was extremely cramped.

The next visit was not until the 3rd of August, when Mr Grimes, assisted by Mrs Williams, carried out the excavation, of the sand pocket to a depth of 3ft 6 ins, which extended from Squares M/n, M/o, N/n and N/o.

In this area more human remains were uncovered, and it became obvious as work progressed, that they had discovered a mass burial site, with seven skeletons in one part alone. The delicate exploration continued for three days, during which time, the couple removed some 3,500 bones, mainly human with some, curiously, belonging to sheep. Of all the human bones recovered, only one had been damaged. One skeleton had been found in a sitting position. The finding of such a large number of human bones in the sand pocket indicated that it had been the best place for burial and it was presumed, that when the pocket had become full, the dwellers buried their dead elsewhere in the cave and covered them with boulders owing to the lack of soil.

The discovery of such a mass grave raised a macabre doubt that the appearance of so many human remains had been the result of a mass murder, but with no proof to substantiate this, it was then thought that the cave could well have been used as a burial chamber, and that when it had become a dwelling, the last occupants had been unaware of that fact when they had inadvertently built their fires over a burial place, which would account for the burnt bones.

It was in square T/f that the most startling discovery was made. Apart from the 57 human bones and numerous fragments of skull bones of 4 adults, were ones belonging to 8 children. Examination of their teeth revealed that their ages ranged mostly from 6–7 years. Oddly, there was a predominance of skull bones.

The human bones were taken to the garage of the nearby *Gwyn Arms*, where they were cleaned and laid out on long trestles. Their discovery had generated an enormous amount of interest in the locality, and it was estimated that a total of 3,000 people arrived to see them.

During the viewing, an amusing piece of 'skulduggery' was reported when one mischievous individual, person unknown, took away a skull and, under the cover of darkness, placed it on a neighbour's doorstep so it would be found when the daily milk was collected in the morning. One can only guess the reaction of the neighbour and that the joker had achieved the surprise he or she intended.

The collection of bones was then taken to the National Museum in Cardiff, to be examined by its Assistant Keeper of Zoology, Mr L. F. Cowley. He reported that they belonged to at least twelve individuals, both male and female. After the last of the bones had been removed from the sand pocket, pieces of a bucket-shaped urn from the Bronze Age were found among the boulders, as well as a variety of objects which were instrumental in dating the bones and certainly made the excavation all the more exciting. These included:

(a) A Roman silver Sesterius coin of the Trajan period (90 –117 AD).

(b) An iron finger ring measuring 13 x 10 mm. The bezel had been set with a paste imitation of a sardonyx which had a red upper surface. This was dated to the 2nd Century.

It is interesting to note, that during the Roman period, iron finger rings were also worn as wedding rings and were considered extremely fashionable.

(c) A fine specimen of a Roman 'Dolphin' brooch, 73 mm (nearly 3 inches long). There were traces of an iron spring pin. Its middle was grooved, with a row of raised dots down either side. The cup-like foot held some kind of setting. There were no traces of tinning.

Brooches of this type were fairly common, and a stumpy 66 mm example is now in the Newport Museum. The brooch was thought to belong to the middle of the 2nd century.

(d) A small fragment of a bone ring.

(e) Part of an iron ring, smaller than above, which had traces of a glass setting.

(f) A single shard from a 4th century flagon.

Outside the grave area:

At a depth of 2ft 6 ins, in an earth filled crevice between the boulders which had been held together by the stalagmite boss, the archaeologists came across their most astonishing finds to date, which made them wonder how they came to be in the cave.

They included:

(a) A strap terminal made of bronze which was 1½ ins/39 mm long. It consisted of a triangle which terminated into a disc. 16 mm in diameter, the disc still bore traces of turquoise enamel.

These ornaments were worn by the military and were sometimes called 'dress fasteners'. Early Roman in origin, the terminal was dated between 66–111 AD.

(b) A circular, bronze seal-box, measuring 23 mm overall, was complete with its lid.

A common Roman type, these boxes contained blocks of wax and were used by high ranking military officers or local officials for sealing dispatches. The lid tops were closed by string which had been attached to the base and passed through two slots in the sides of the boxes. Remarkably, the lid was still hinged to the box and, despite centuries of neglect, it was in good working order. The decoration of engraved dots and circles was considered unusual for this item. It had probably been enamelled or had niello: a black composition of sulphur with silver, lead or copper, which was used to fill in the engraved lines which had been cut into silver or metal work. There was no trace of tinning, which was more commonly applied to such objects. Some brownish-grey dust, found in the interior of the box, was tested by heating and gave off a waxy, resinous odour, proving that it had originally contained wax.

Most surprising find of all, was the discovery of part of a steelyard arm, also cast in bronze and made during the Roman period. Oval in shape, it measured 76 mm. It was estimated that it would have been 92 mm long before it was broken. These objects were usually suspended from a loop and used as weighing scales. This object had been graduated to weigh objects in Roman weights of up to 20 *librae*, (6.5 kg), with the upper edge weighing items by *unciae*, up to 5 *librae* 10 *unciae*, and the lower edge graduated every 5 *librae*. Closer examination revealed filing marks on the steelyard which suggested that it had been repaired on two occasions. It was thought, that as a weakness had been found in the metal at the time of manufacture, a slot had been cut and filled in with fresh metal.

Other finds in neighbouring squares included:

(1) In square M/n a large Roman Trumpet brooch was found. Length 63 mm. The mouth of the bow was outlined in a white metal band with a band of the same material around the middle. It also had a ring of white

Roman Finds: Dolphin and Trumpet Brooches & Serpent bracelet Seal Box, Coin and Omega Brooch

metal around the enamel setting, which was dark royal blue with bronze spots around a central jade green disc.

Brooches of this type were said to be fairly common in Britain, but were rarer on the Continent. Examples have been found at Caerleon and Caerwent.

(b) A pennular brooch of the Omega type (almost circular in shape and resembling the Greek letter). Usually made of bronze, this specimen was made of brass. Diameter 35 mm. These brooches came into existence during the 2nd Century and were of Iberian origin. It probably found its way to the cave from *Y Gaer,* since the Fort there had been occupied by the Second Augustian Legion, which consisted of 3,000 Spanish Cavalry. This type of brooch was considered rare in Britain. It is now displayed in the National Museum, Cardiff.

(c) Another Trumpet brooch was found, in square P/h., 62 mm long with an iron pin. It had a raised 'late' Celtic scroll-work design. It was dated to the 2nd century.

(d) A bronze bow brooch of fine golden bronze, 63 mm long with a small decorative feature on the head. Dated not later than 100 AD.

(e) A shard to match the one found in the grave area, which had come from the same 4th Century flagon. In total, the fragments of sixteen different vessels were found.

Then came a surprising find. Among the Bronze Age and Roman fragments were two shards which seem to indicate that there had also been some thirteenth century activity in the cave.

The shards came from:

(a) Part of the upper body of a jar or pitcher with an external green glaze, similar to one found at Kidwelly Castle and dated from 1275-1320, and

(b) The rim of a cooking pot of ill-fired, gritty, drab ware with a reddish surface. This piece was again compared with those found at Kidwelly Castle and dated 1106-1275.

Greatly encouraged by these finds, excavation was carried out in the rest of the cave, and at a depth of 8 inches in square M/m, a 13½- inch-long, bronze dirk or rapier was found embedded at an angle of 45 degrees with its tip projecting into a filled up rabbit burrow. As the bones of a rabbit were found close by, it was believed that the unfortunate animal had impaled itself upon the blade.

The rapier, which could have been used for carving up meat, or as a short thrusting sword, had a broad flat surface with concave edges which appeared to have suffered a good deal of corrosion. The butt had deep recesses for a rivet on each side, for attaching to a handle, and there was also a damaged rivet hole between the recesses, which suggested that the rapier had been repaired. There was no sign of the handle. It had probably been made of wood and had disintegrated over the centuries. The rapier, which was dated to the Middle Bronze Age (1500-1000 BC), was an exciting archaeological find. Only eleven have been found in Wales, at places such as Llansannor in Glamorganshire, Mynydd Wyddgen in Montgomeryshire, and Drygarn Fawr, Breconshire. (This is now in the Brecon Museum). One was also found at Cwm Du, near Brecon, and another specimen was unearthed on a site in Beddgelert. The rapier from Yr Ogof is now in on display at the National Museum of Wales. These rapiers preceded the locally produced leaf-shaped swords which were later to become more common throughout Britain. The origin of the leaf-shaped sword was traced to the Hungarian Plain during the second century.

On the stalagmite floor in the same square they found a bronze awl: a small pointed tool which could have been used for piercing leather for thonging. These awls are mainly Early Bronze Age in date, but it was supposed that by the second century some change in form may have occurred.

Most surprising of all was the discovery of a pure gold bead, only 8 mm in diameter and 6 mm high. There was no evidence that the bead had been worn as an ornament, but similar beads had been known to adorn looped armlets and torcs. In comparing it with other beads found in excavations elsewhere, it was dated between 1050-850 BC. Looking as new and shiny as the day it was made, the bead can also be seen at the National Museum in Cardiff.

Another item found which could have been worn as an ornament was a dog's tooth. It had been pierced for attaching to an amulet. These were worn as charms to ward off evil spirits. A similar amulet was found with British/Romano material at a site in Yorkshire.

On the same stalagmite floor they found domestic implements which gave a clearer picture of the lives of our Bronze Age dwellers. They were:

(a) A primitive form of a bone weaving comb which had been made from an ox's bone and had eight teeth. As it had been badly damaged, it could not be dated accurately. The only other weaving comb to be found in Britain came from the Middle Bronze Age settlement in Dorset, but this

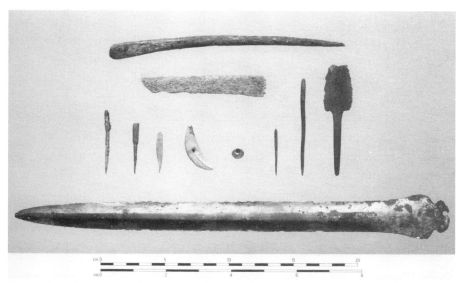

Relics from the Bronze Age showing the Spatula, Bone razor and pins, gold bead and bronze razor and rapier
(Reproduced by kind permission of The National Museums and Galleries of Wales)

Tableau of Archaeologists at work during the 1938 excavations

Beyond The Lakes
(Reproduced by kind permission of Mr Ashford Price)

specimen differed from the Dorset one.

(b) A double sided comb made from the antler of a deer was also found. On the one side, the teeth were 23 mm long and closely spaced, while on the other side, the teeth had been cut diagonally. Interestingly, they bore marks of having combed long and tangled hair.

(c) Another bone implement was a spatulate tool, 184 mm (about 6 inches long) and pointed at one end. Multiple diagonal markings on both surfaces of the broad end could be seen, which indicated that it had been well used, probably for smoothing the surfaces of pots before firing.

(d) A tanged bronze razor, 91 mm long and 6 mm wide. Its edges had been damaged by corrosion. The razor was found under some human remains.

In addition to the silver Sesterius coin found in the grave, two other Roman coins were found beneath the large slab of rock once it had been removed by a small explosive charge. The coins appeared to have come from a linen bag, but very little of the cloth remained, although one coin was still adhering to the material, which had been stained by its corrosion. One coin was a Denarius, from the time of Hadrian, AD 11, and the other was a Vespesian As, AD 3-72. In Roman values, a Sesterius equalled 2 Asses or a quarter of a Denarius. What remained of the bag was sent to Mr G. Ellis, Assistant Keeper of Botany at the National Museum of Wales, for scientific analysis. First, the fibres were boiled, to see if they were made of animal fibre. This test was discounted when the fibres did not turn yellow, as would then have been the case; but when the fibres were subjected to a weak solution of iodine and potassium iodine, the fibres immediately turned blue when 70% of sulphuric acid was added, proving that the fibres were of vegetable origin. Microscopic examination then confirmed that the bag had been made of flax.

Another decorative item was a snake-head bracelet, 60 mm in diameter, with the 'serpent's' eyes made by engraved circles. The bracelet was found in two parts, broken by fallen debris which had caused one half to fly off in a different direction, but this was later found not too far away. The hoop showed evidence that efforts had been made to make the circle smaller. A stone mould for these bracelets was found during excavations in Caerwent and is now in the Newport Museum.

The possession of so many rich objects for so humble an abode puzzled the archaeologists, especially the seal box and the weighing device, which would have had no practical use for the dwellers. It made them wonder: was it loot and they had been a band of robbers who had been keeping track of Roman movements on the road below? Or had the objects come by other means? As it had been the practise of the native population to rummage among the Roman forts when they had become abandoned, therefore, our cave dwellers could have acquired what the Legionnaires had left behind when they moved north to build Hadrian's wall.

For instance, Mortimer Wheeler discovered that the Roman Camp at Coelbren, in particular, had been abandoned after only a short occupation, and that the re-building in stone of Yr Gaer, Brecon, was interrupted about AD 120, and it was partially burnt down before it was abandoned altogether. Many of these Welsh forts remained unoccupied or desolate for more than half a century until, during the reign of Septimus Severus, the partial re-occupation of the Principality ushered in the second phase of the Roman occupation.

It was decided, after examining the finds, that the Bronze Age objects did not suggest a prolonged occupation, and appeared to confirm that it took place sometime between the eleventh and the beginning of the eighth century BC. It was also thought that the cave had been in use over a long period of time which had spanned some eighty years, with the date of the Roman occupation taking place during the Antonine period, in the second to the third century.

The positions of the various burials were curious, but taking into account the accumulation of so many boulders in the cave, the only suitable areas had been those where objects had been found. The finding of so many scattered bones, however, was blamed on the action of the stream causing disturbance to the burials, and, of course, on the inhabitants themselves for clearing the floor area. It was thought that the movement of water had also been the reason why so many of the Bronze Age relics had become mixed with the British/Romano finds.

In the 'grave', it appeared that some of the children's skulls had moved since burial, but this was not regarded as unusual, since sand was subject to some natural movement of its own.

Mr L. F. Cowley, from the Department of Zoology at the National Museum, examined all the human bones found and estimated that 31 individuals had been discovered in the body of the cave, of which 12 were probably adults, with the remaining 19 being immature individuals of various ages. To these figures were added the remains found in Square T/f, making 40 individuals in all, comprising 14 adults and 26 non adults.

Following the discovery of so many human bones, it was decided that Yr Ogof's name should be changed to Ogof-yr-Esgyrn, (The Cave of Bones), simplified to **Bone Cave,** and this is how we refer to this solitary but exciting cave today. Of all the bones found, there was, however, one which was of great interest. It was the bone of a red deer and thought to be at least 7,000 years old.

Having excavated as much of the cave as they could in such a cramped area, the party left the scene in the hope of recommencing at a later date. With such a successful excavation having been achieved, the cave was no longer a mystery that had made people wonder what was hidden inside.

The richness and diversity of its finds proved that it had been part of Wales's historic past and had given an important insight into two separate yet distinct periods in time, providing valuable evidence as to how man had lived and progressed, especially in the art of making objects of adornment and practical use. The finds stirred the imagination, and with so many of its secrets revealed, one wondered what else there was to find.

Cathedral Cave: 1953 Exploration

The original entrance into Cathedral Cave, seen behind the black iron railings on the right hand side of the cave's entrance, was probably known to the Morgan Brothers, but it possibly appeared too tiny and too difficult to investigate. It was not explored until December 1953, when a party from The South Wales Caving Club got through to reach the enormous cavern we see today. Cavers, Edward Aslett, David Hunt, Bill Clarke, Lewis Railton and John Truman greatly contributed to the work which finally led to the discovery, said to be the richest in geological history.

This new discovery was first called Tunnel Cave because of its extremely long entrance. It was first discovered when members of The South Wales Caving Club cleared away the mass of boulders which had created a dam across its 4ft wide entrance. As it was higher than the passage, the wet weather had tended to seal it off and had made entry difficult. After they had cleared away the obstruction, the opening eventually led to a long passage which wound for a distance of 150 feet and was, in many places, half filled with water and debris that had fallen from the roof. Even so, a strong draught was felt and this gave the explorers hope that there was an even larger opening beyond.

On a warm day, on the 1st August, 1953, they decided to risk removing some of the boulders with a small charge of explosives, but a cloud of smoke drove the explorers out. In the cramped conditions, it took many weekends to clear away the debris, but by the Sunday before Christmas a black space was seen. As the opening was still too small to get through, the cavers decided to leave it for the time being and concentrate their energies on exploring the main caves.

Another opportunity presented itself on Sunday, 27th December, when a small explosive charge produced results and caver, John Truman, found himself standing inside a small chamber with its floor covered with chunks of broken rock. He was joined by Lewis Railton and the rest of the men. Then, through a wisp of smoke, another wall could be seen, 15 feet away, which Railton followed for a hundred feet. At its end he found he had reached a floor of fine white gravel. When the rest of the smoke had cleared, he was overwhelmed by the enormity of the passage he had entered. It was a thrilling find.

Joined by the others, the men soon found themselves walking down the wide passage we know today, with hundreds of golden coloured straws hanging from a ceiling that eventually rose from 10 to 45 feet high. The feeling of space was enormous. Halfway down, and under the right hand wall, a stream crossed a wide shingle bank where a small passage was visible under the water. This was known as **The Flood Rising.** There was also an approximate one foot depth of water which extended for about 20 feet, but this was eventually pumped away.

To the right of the chamber, they found a balcony with a tight aven leading to a small one containing a fine crystal pool. A very rare find was a nest of cave pearls, formed when drips of water had made hollows in the rock in which there were small grains of sand or gravel. The constant agitation of the water, which was rich in lime, encrusted the grains with calcite and thus created pearls in the same way as sea pearls are formed with small grains of sand.

When the explorers had reached a T-junction they were faced with an even larger passage, **(St. Paul's Chamber),** and where the stream widened, banks of mud two feet thick were decoratively patterned with 'roses' caused by drips of water falling from the high ceiling.

On going the other way, the entrants soon found themselves

scrambling over mountainous piles of fallen rock which made progress extremely slow and arduous. On top, the scene changed dramatically when the cavern narrowed considerably, varying between 3-8 feet wide, although the roof remained 15-20 feet high. The floor was strewn with slabs of rock that had broken off the walls. Progress along this stretch was again difficult. They removed whatever obstacles they could and noted the irregular fissures in the floor. When they came to an awkward looking 3 metre drop, they decided 'to call it a day' and, thinking that their comrades would be worrying about them, they returned to the entrance. When they emerged, a large crowd had already gathered and was anxiously waiting for them. Excitedly, they related what they had found.

As members of the Club had been 'paying their last respects' to an old friend and fellow member, the newly discovered 45-foot-high cavern was named Davy Price's Hall in his memory. The finding of such a large cavern had great significance in caving terms. It was the largest ever found in the country and was a tremendous coup for both Dan yr Ogof and for the members of The South Wales Caving Club. As the lights from the explorers' helmets had been insufficient to assess the full value of the 'Hall' as a tourist attraction, Mr Ashford Price, Dan yr Ogof's Development Manager, contacted British Oxygen with a view to borrowing some gas lights to view the Cave properly. Once the lights had been set down its entire length, its vastness and beauty was fully revealed, especially the different colours in the rock and the great number of straws hanging from the ceiling, proving beyond doubt that Dan yr Ogof had yet another attraction to offer its visitors.

A survey was carried out by the National Coal Board, which was completed after many weekends of braving the cold. The task of making an opening wide enough for the public to walk through was given to Foraky Limited, a mining concern in Nottingham, but as the only method of doing this was to blast a way through the rock, concern was expressed about the delicate formations which could not withstand the violent vibrations caused by the blasting. 'One little mistake,' the Manager was quoted as saying, 'and everything would be destroyed.' But in the expert opinion of Mr Larry Phillips, Foraky's Contracts Engineer, no such doubt existed. With the aid of a 3,000 watt lamp he called Big Bertha, he had arrived in November to examine the cave. Under the expert guidance of ICI, the correct explosives were carefully placed in the rock, and not a single formation was damaged following the blast, or whilst men had been working to within fifteen feet of the delicate formations.

The final breakthrough into Tunnel Cave came on the last day of 1970, after 10,000 cubic feet of rock had been removed. An expert team of eight ex-miners then began the enormous task of clearing away the rubble inside the 'Hall'. The estimated 1,200 tons of rock that had been cleared was broken up and later used as a base for a concrete path down the entire length of the cave. In order to keep the natural character of the interior, the pathway was kept to one side, allowing the boulders on the right to be left undisturbed. The path was just wide enough for a car to pass along, and the workmen tested it with a Mini the next day.

Owing to the cave's size, it was considered that something more powerful than the 350 light bulbs used in the main show-cave was required for lighting. Consequently, a mile and a half of electrical cables were laid for what turned out to be a complicated electrical system, but making it possible for lights to be switched off when not in use. This reduces the risk of moss and algae growing anywhere in the cave.

The entire operation, from survey to completion, had taken just over four months and the cave was presented to the general public at a grand opening. For commercial purposes, the 'Hall' became known as **Cathedral Cave** because of its cathedral-like proportions.

The project had not been without its problems. At the start, when excavating half-way up the disused quarry face, below the natural entrance, the roof fell in when the workmen encountered a solid wall of limestone after six weeks' hard work, and this caused them to stop after only 21 feet. The solution was to follow as closely as possible the beds over the natural entrance. Then, there was the problem of getting a path over the mud close to the sump. On one occasion, the mechanical dumper almost disappeared in the sea of mud, along with its protesting driver. It also transpired, that as the stones for the concrete base were continually disappearing into the mud, it was taking ten tons of stone just to complete three yards of pathway. The path was completed in four weeks.

To recreate the waterfalls which existed inside the cave up until the Ice Age, the Management consulted an engineering firm in Pontardawe about how to pump up water from the lake and to send it gushing 40 feet back into the lake. The waterfalls had once been fed by the river Haffes, but when the river was diverted to a new course, they became dry. The fluting they left behind in the soft limestone is the only evidence that the falls had ever existed. In consultation with the firm, the exact amount of water going over the falls at that time had to be established, so as to give greater accuracy to the scene.

The pumps had also to be silent, and to keep the overall effect as natural as possible, the water was pumped up through the natural fissures in the rock. The waterfalls spring into action at the press of a hidden button, and are an attractive feature enjoyed by all.

Because of its dome-like roof, the cavern containing these waterfalls is called **St. Paul's.** The Cathedral Cave has also been the scene of many celebrations and festive events. Each December, Father Christmas makes a special visit here to delight the scores of children who make a special visit to see him, either in the company of their parents, or with fellow classmates, who arrive by the coach load. For their enjoyment, the Cave is decorated for the occasion with brightly coloured lights and Christmas scenes. They will see Polystyrene penguins floating on 'ice packs' that drift on the streams and a brightly lit Fairyland Grotto where Santa hands out his gifts. No child leaves without receiving one.

Romance also comes to The Cathedral Cave. Granted a licence in 1997 to perform weddings which are officiated by the local Registrar, couples come here to exchange their vows beneath the domed ceiling of St. Paul's Chamber. They can be married to the music of their choice, and some have even had a full choir to perform at the ceremony. Couples can also choose from many wedding themes, from the traditional to the Gothic. To create a romantic atmosphere, candles and flowers are placed upon the lake. Some couples have even come from abroad to be married here, including a couple from Japan.

Filming has also been carried out in the Cave. An episode of the popular BBC Series *Dr Who* was filmed here in May, 1978, with the cave providing a perfect setting for the instalment entitled *The Pirate Planet*. Tom Baker, the star of the show, later obliged the management by accepting their invitation to open the newly constructed Jubilee Passage in the main show-cave.

Then a Pop Group, Depeche Mode, looking for an unusual location for their video to promote their latest single, '*Love in Itself*', arrived here on the recommendation of The British Tourist Board when they were looking for somewhere which would guarantee them 'peace and quiet'. They arrived with a full back-up team of technicians who provided the special lighting effects for the video. This was the first time that a popular singing group had used such a location and they were said to have returned to London pleased with the result of their experience.

Another unusual event took place during the Mid Wales and Countryside Festival, when a specially commissioned dance was performed by the Cardiff-based group Dance Alive, in the light of a thousand candles.

During the 25th Anniversary celebrations of the caves' opening, Dr David Bellamy, the popular Botanist and Television Celebrity, visited Dan yr Ogof after an eighteen year lapse, and was said to be 'particularly impressed' with the Cathedral Cave and called it 'One of the Seven Wonders of Wales'. The Cathedral Cave is also noted for its acoustic qualities and has been a popular venue with local choirs. In May 1988, ninety members of the Ystradgynlais Male Voice Choir, with thirty members of the town's Silver Band, played to visitors during the Festival of Rock, and as many as a thousand people stayed to listen to the Choir. The Festival was part of a four-month programme of activities.

In August 1990, a 35-strong mixed choir from Moscow, having accepted an invitation to Ystradgynlais from the Male Voice Choir, paid a visit to Dan yr Ogof, and, after being given a tour of Cathedral Cave, gave a special performance of Russian songs, providing yet another pleasant and unique occasion.

As a result of *perestroika,* which greatly improved the freedom of movement for Soviet citizens, the Retro Choir from Moscow became the first to visit Wales, and during their ten-day tour, they stayed as guests in the homes of the Ystradgynlais Male Voice Choir, with whom they also sang at a specially arranged concert. During their stay in the town, they also gave a performance to a packed St. Cynog's Church, and sang to an appreciative audience at the local Maesydderwen School.

The Russians, many of whom spoke English, struck up a friendly relationship with the local people and expressed their delight at being in the area. They especially enjoyed their visit to Dan yr Ogof and being allowed to photograph many of the outstanding formations in the Cathedral Cave, which gave them lasting memories of their visit.

Their visit coincided with August's '*Music in the Mountains*' Charity Fete, in aid of guide dogs for the blind, at Dan yr Ogof. Promoted by the Brecon Beacons Tourist Association and supported by the Development Board for Rural Wales, the activities included displays of folk and country dancing, with the musical entertainment provided by the Band of the Royal Regiment of Wales. During the event, members of the Choir participated at the Craft and Rural Displays Section by selling good quality wooden and embroidered items which they had made, and these proved to be good buys. The wooden items, I recall, such as the decorative spoons and boxes, were all brightly painted, as were the Russian dolls – all colourful reminders of a successful visit. Someone in the costume of a Russian bear became a mascot of the choir and delighted the children at the Fete.

On arrival inside the cave, present day visitors are immediately impressed by its size and the glowing colour of the hundreds of golden straws hanging from the ceiling. Soon after entering, the visitor's attention is drawn

Cathedral Cave: Tableau of Cave Artists

to the left, where, behind a high iron grille, are tableaux of life-sized figures recreating events in the lives of the people who once inhabited caves some 30,000 years ago. A recorded commentary tells the story of each tableau, starting with a dramatic clap of thunder, followed by special lighting effects to recreate flashes of lightning, to produce the atmospheric conditions of a storm raging outside.

67

Then, as the story unfolds, each tableau is lit to illustrate the part of the story being told, such as a burial, with members of a Neanderthal family grouped around an open grave in which weapons and food have been laid. As is also shown in the tableau, the arms and legs of the corpse are bound, so that its spirit does not return to haunt the living. Another form of burial which took place during that time was when the body was left outside the cave until the flesh had been removed by weather or animal. The skeleton was then placed in a grave.

One tableau shows a small group of cave artists wall painting, with one using a small tube to blow the coloured pigment on to the wall. Close by is the figure of a Shaman, or Medicine Man, seemingly performing a ritual dance. There has been no evidence that cave artists had been at work in the Bone Cave. Opposite, attention is drawn to the enormous boulders which remain in the same position as they were found.

A little further on, in a hollowed out rock are specimens of the tiny salamanders which are found in European caves. The models are twice their normal size and their lack of colour is due to them living permanently in the dark. The small display of different kinds of rocks and minerals from other parts of the caves are of some geological and scientific interest.

As the passage narrows, it turns again to take the visitor past the little lake with its clear reflections of the surrounding rock, and then past the stream fed by the continuous flow of water cascading down the walls. The distinctive ridging in the orange coloured rock, left behind by the original waterfall, is now called **The Organ Pipes,** and as the sound of pastoral music swells throughout the cave, one has the same feeling of peace as one finds inside a real cathedral. Along this stretch there are some delightful images carved in the golden coloured stalagmites, with many taking on human form and creating unusual pictures that stir the imagination. There are also caving scenes, with life-sized models clinging to ropes suspended from the ceiling to show modern day caving techniques. Another model, complete with breathing apparatus, is about to 'explore' a narrow streamway.

Beneath a much lower ceiling, the path follows the stream flowing on the left hand side of the cave, and, after turning again, it brings the visitor into full view of **St. Paul's Chamber,** with its two waterfalls splashing noisily into the lake.

Because the path alongside the lake was continually flooding, the Management decided to block it off and build a ramp to take visitors to an observation platform so they could view the lake and the entire Chamber safely from an elevated position.

Now, with the problem of the flooding solved, the Management reversed its decision, and by way of a path leading down from the observation platform, it has allowed the visitor to walk beside the lake once more. This new railed pathway takes the visitor behind the waterfalls which provides an extra thrill of being able to walk inbetween the cascading waters without getting wet.

St. Paul's is not without its own pleasing display of formations. Above the lake, beneath an opening where a waterfall once emerged, is a long flow of calcite which looks as though the water had turned into a solid mass the moment it went over the edge. The stalactites hanging from this formation extend downwards like long tenrils to meet the small group of stalagmites at the edge of the lake. These are now but a touch away. Here too, on looking upwards into the domed roof, visitors can have a greater appreciation of the Chamber's massive height and the vastness of its great expanse. Scrutiny of the roof reveals an interesting array of different formations which include small 'curtains' and multi coloured stalactites.

The 'dome' also shows signs of scalloping – impressions of whirlpools in the rock – and there are signs of seashells fossilised in the walls with traces of coral, giving evidence that the cave once lay beneath the sea, between 200-230 millions years ago, when the tides also caused rippling to the walls.

At the far end of the path is a narrow 'keyhole' opening through which is another mile of passageways explored in 1954. Here, a 'No Entry' sign warns visitors not to stray from the path, as to do so would be extremely dangerous. However, the path continues to meander around the Chamber and takes visitors pass the newly created mini lake in which the reflected illuminations provide yet another stunning spectacle.

One is almost reluctant to leave the stirring atmosphere of **St. Paul's Chamber.** Its magic is a lasting one and entices the visitor to return. Outside, at the top of the Geological Trail, visitors are greeted by another inspiring sight: a clear view of the meadows and mountain peaks on the other side of the valley.

Further Explorations: 1954

A further visit into the newly explored Davy Price's Hall (Cathedral Cave) was made on the 2nd January, 1954, when a large party split into two groups to explore the divided passages leading away from where they had left off.

The group which took the right hand passage reported that the top part was no more than a large tube connected to the lower by a fissure of only two feet wide. This gave way to a small passage with crystal pools and a calcite floor, rising sharply, then dipping before changing into a more spacious passage with a sandy floor.

On the right hand side, a boulder-filled passage ran downwards to a fine chamber containing some very soft, white calcite straws, many of which were 8ft long and some even extending from roof to floor. In a gour pool were some helictites growing in the water. This picturesque cave was given the name **Christmas Grotto.** The main passage continued for several hundred feet before opening out into a wide aven, about seventy feet high, near the top of which was another passage. Beyond this aven, aptly named Steeple Aven, a narrow rift led to a small chamber, from which another rift passage led off. Further on, the party had to remove a pile of boulders before emerging through a 30ft high passage running north to south. At its southerly end they again found their way blocked with boulders and sand, but they were convinced, that beyond the pileup, there were many more caves to explore. The passage, which they named Switchback Passage, ended in a spacious chamber which had two or three of its exits completely covered with calcite formations, leaving only one way out through a narrow fissure.

At one place a crowbar had to be used to make a way through the barrier of stalagmite to enable them to crawl past. Eventually, they found themselves entering what they called **Final Chamber,** and it was here that they ended this visit.

During their next visit, the party returned to the spot where they had finished their first exploration, and entered a passage only 10 feet high. They found that it contained many orange-coloured formations with 3ft long straws. When the roof lowered, the only way they could proceed was by crawling over the boulders. At a point where it was thought that it would be impossible to continue, the passage suddenly led into another large chamber, with an amazing feature of a 60ft long stalagmite mass coming down an aven. They climbed up this treacherous slope and entered a smaller chamber with some fine gours. There were two avens in the roof but, on investigation, these did not appear to lead anywhere.

There was also a solid slope of stalagmite on the left, with a traverse to the upper part of the main aven which interested them. On reaching the traverse, they found a steep slope of stalagmite-covered boulders, some 40ft high, which provided them with another impressive spectacle. Masses of stalactite hung from the roof and effectively blocked what must have been a fair sized passage. In the other direction, a high passage was also blocked, but in this instance by boulders.

The overall height of this aven, called Cascade Aven, was estimated at a staggering 140ft, and a climb to within 20ft of the roof was achieved. This section of the cave is now known as **The Eastern Series.**

The second party, consisting of only two members, took the left-hand fork at the junction, to enter one of the most impressive but difficult passages ever encountered. Four hundred yards long and 40 feet high, it was so narrow that walking along its floor was practically impossible. The only way forward was by finding footholds in the steep walls on either side and projecting themselves forward with their hands. The high roof greatly accentuated the narrowness of the passage, but when it started to diminish, the passage became even narrower and, with several hairpin bends to negotiate, it was only marginally possible to go along, but they pressed on to see what lay beyond.

After a hundred yards or so, they encountered a small waterfall pouring down from the roof. It disappeared as a stream in between the boulders. Then, they saw a parallel passage through a gap in the wall, and on the floor of this was a 'pot', thirty-two feet deep, which they called the **Thirty-Two Pot.** Intrigued to know what lay at the bottom, they climbed down and found a large sandy chamber, about 20ft wide. They also encountered a stream which was believed to be the same one they had met in the previous passage. This, too, disappeared among the boulders.

Without a rope, which was essential if they were to scale a difficult climb, and exhausted after being constantly on the move for some hours, the men decided to continue their exploration the next day. With their watches telling them that it was already 10 o'clock in the night, it was considered time they got back to the surface.

This section, known as **Western Series,** is considered by cavers to be the most difficult ever encountered in South Wales.

As a result of these explorations, it was reported that about a mile of new passages had been discovered and that their general direction tended to go towards the Sink at Waun Fignen Felen. Further exploration was, unfortunately, bedevilled by continuous rain, which flooded both the Llynfell and Tawe rivers, causing stream banks to collapse under the sheer weight of water. It was recorded, during that first weekend in August, starting at midday on the Sunday and lasting until the afternoon of Monday, 2nd August, 3.04 inches of rain had fallen. As a result, the entrance to 'Tunnel Cave' was again blocked by fallen boulders, which had to be cleared. With this accomplished, the smaller pieces of debris could then be naturally washed away.

During the following weekends, members of the Caving Club were back on site and the traverse between the First and Second Cascade of **Cascades Aven** had been successfully climbed and so had the Second Cascade.

During the late summer of 1974, some more remarkable discoveries were made when, by accident, three cavers found sizeable caverns at the extreme end of Tunnel Cave. Cavers Mike Haselden, Barney Evans and Susan Salter had climbed up the slopes of Twyn Spratt (to the right of Dan yr Ogof) , in search of Pwll Dwfn (Deep Pool), with the intention of scaling its impressive pitches. Having entered what they thought was the correct place, they were completely baffled at not being able to find them. The system in which they found themselves was not consistent with the guide book. Even after making a thorough search of the vicinity, the pitches of Pwll Dwfn remained elusive to them. They came to the conclusion that they had found an entry into an entirely different system. Below, they could hear the sound of water, and descent of the first cascade was made by rope. But as the approach to the second cascade was rather steep and exposed, they fixed a wire traverse on the right hand ledge, to enable them to descend with safety. This manoeuvre finally brought them into a wide opening, which they called Cascades Chamber, and, from there onwards, a low passage took them in a south-easterly direction.

At the end of this passage they encountered a 15ft drop which, to their surprise, took them into a 40ft long chamber. At the far end there was a narrow passage. Although obstructed by a rock fall, the trio pushed through and found themselves in another large cavern, which was approximately 30ft long and 20ft wide, and it became very apparent that the system in which they found themselves was quite a significant one and worth exploring.

On passing through this, they found an extremely long passage which seemed to stretch far into the darkness. In fact, it took them a further 100 feet deeper into the mountain. At its end they came to a short drop and another 40 foot high cave. Here, Barney Evans separated from his two companions, and whilst they went off to explore what has become known as the 35ft Pot Series, he began to search for a possible way forward, and found one behind some boulders.

Next, he found himself standing on a sandy floor and looking down another enormous cavern with delicate straws hanging from its low ceiling.

The chamber he had entered was even larger than the last; 60 feet long and approximately 25 feet at its widest. In its south-western corner was a rift passage, and as this led up to other extensions above, Evans decided not to explore them but to see if the blockage at the far end led anywhere. He was not disappointed. Stooping under a low and unstable-looking roof, he carefully moved the large rock which obstructed his path and scrambled over it to find that there was, indeed, another chamber beyond. Here again, the ceiling was low and richly adorned with a fine collection of straw stalactites. Even the floor provided a pleasing display of mud and crystal 'flowers'. Because of their vulnerability, he had to be extremely careful in passing them.

This beautiful chamber was a spectacular find. It was some 80 feet long, and at its widest point was 50 feet across. It was against its north-western wall that Evans came to another amazing find. There, a group of four stalactites hung down like the tentacles of a gigantic octopus, prompting him to call this strange formation **The Quadrupus.**

But the surprises were not over; looking up, Evans could see that he was standing beneath an aven about fifty feet high and, from all appearances, it led to another aven, at a higher level. His immediate inclination was to scale it, but anxious to share his discoveries with his two companions, he went in search of them.

He found his friends equally excited as to what they had found and, retracing their friend's steps, the pair quickly dubbed the first two chambers **Sandy Chamber** and **Boulder Chamber.** They also named the aven after their friend, and it became known as **Barney's Aven.**

In tackling the aven, the party found a convenient ledge half way up where they could fix the rope to use as a hand line. This enabled them to carry out the most difficult part of the climb which took them up to ceiling height. There, they entered a 20-foot-long, curving passage, which proved extremely tight because its left hand wall was thickly encrusted with stalagmites. Beyond, they met a shorter and less hazardous passage which took them into a small, almost circular cave. This was given the name of

Oxbow Chamber. There, two passages went in different directions, one led northwards, and the other towards the west. They immediately invited exploration, but as time had passed all too quickly, the party reluctantly made for the surface.

It was with a feeling of great achievement that they reached their Camp to tell their colleagues what they had found. This was a source of great interest to their caving companions who suspected that an important connection to Tunnel Cave had been made. The discoveries they made make us realise what wonders lie deep inside the mountain, as from the surface, one would never suspect that such a labyrinth of passages exist beneath the grass. Unfortunately, because of other caving commitments and the onset of winter, the original trio were unable to return to the scene of their discoveries that autumn, but arrived there on the 25th May, 1975, to explore the upper passages.

On this occasion, the party were joined by other members of the Club, and Barney Evans took Paul Follet to Oxbow Chamber with the intention of exploring those passages leading from it.

Taking the western exit, a short crawl led them into a 100-foot-long passage which suddenly turned southwards in a 'wishbone' like manner. This twisted and turned for an incredible 600 feet, and along the way, they had to keep close to the wall to avoid treading on some delicate formations.

This incredible passage took them along a narrow rift and then through a fearsome-looking place with stalagmites piercing the blackness like the teeth of a prehistoric monster. This particular section was nicknamed **The Jaws of Hell**. Still twisting, the passage then produced some fine looking straws, then more stalactites, all making the long walk worthwhile, until, at last, the ground sloped downwards into a picturesque grotto which was considered to be the showpiece of this extraordinary passage. Beyond the grotto, they encountered their first glimpse of water which curved in a semicircular fashion into the dim distance.

Once through this canal, they spotted an opening which was extremely tight, but once they had squeezed through, they found that it forked out in two directions. Taking the left hand passage, the men experienced another pleasant surprise. For, as they reached the end of this 80 foot long extension, which tapered to a point, they were confronted with two enormous stalagmites that almost reached the ceiling. They named the end of this passage **Termination Point**, and it was here that they ended the day.

To keep the momentum of this exciting exploration going, the original trio returned here the following day, with fellow caver Tony Mintram, who then photographed all the best formations. Together, the party went as far as **Termination Point,** where Evans proudly showed them the two enormous stalagmites. Then, as a tribute to the men who found them, the formations were promptly dubbed **Paul and Barnabus.**

Deciding to examine the north passage in Oxbow Chamber, the party climbed 12 feet over some unstable rocks and, after squeezing through another tight and twisting passage for a distance of 60 feet, a pool led them into a little, almost circular chamber. It was at its western wall that they saw an aven which rose another 20 feet above them.

Curious to know where it led, ropes were brought into play as Haselden first climbed to the top. After squeezing himself down a short, tight passage, he made the most spectacular discovery of the day. For there, in a large pool and glowing in the light of his lamp, were hundreds of translucent cave pearls of every dimension. It was a most thrilling sight and was regarded as an outstanding speleological discovery.

Joined by the rest of the party, they passed over the pearls with extreme care and followed the tight passage beyond but, after 70 feet, it terminated in a series of minute solution tubes, which were then examined to their limits.

The opening they found 4 feet up on the right hand wall of the western passage and leading out of Oxbow Chamber was also investigated. After an arduous crawl of about 50 feet, the passage opened out into a tiny circular cave which revealed yet another surprise. At their feet was a delicate crystal floor. This eventually led to **Pearl Aven.**

On the 9th of August, Haselden returned to this section of Tunnel Cave with Sue Salter, Colin Salter and Roger Smith, the last two of whom were anxious to share in the amazing discoveries. And after leaving Sue Salter and Roger Smith at the Canal, Haselden and Colin went on to **Paul and Barnabus.**

Whilst there, they decided to examine the opening found close to the canal and, after an easy climb of less than 20 feet, they entered a narrow, water-worn passage with a hardened mud floor. It was an interesting discovery; the walls were covered with picturesque formations of calcite and many small straws hanging from the ceiling. The short passage ended in a narrow rift with a connecting hole to a lower complex. However, the intriguing sound of running water coming from a right hand passage enticed Haselden to venture into it. Half way along, a 20ft waterfall was encountered, but in order to reach the opening out of which the water tumbled, they had to climb up the vertical rift to roof level. It was an arduous climb and, to make matters more difficult, there were sharp protrusions to overcome. Loose boulders also contributed to the hazard of climbing up the narrow rift, and these had to be cleared with every foothold taken.

Leading the party along the water filled passage, Haselden took some time to get through the vice-like grip of the vertical squeeze at the top, but once through, he met the stream passage again, but at a higher level. He followed it for some 30ft., but because it was body-tight, he found that he was plugging up the flow of water with his body. He could see that the way onwards was so overgrown with formations and calcified boulders that further progress was impossible.

Downstream, too, the passage soon diminished into an incredibly narrow tube, and the water vanished through a narrow space between two rocks. Disappointed, the party had to concede that further exploration there would be 'diabolically dangerous' and they abandoned the idea.

At a later date, the high level extension above Barney's Aven was explored, and this was reached by swinging over the exposed aven by way of a rope hooked into the rift above it. This procedure was called Pit and Pendulum, but like the rest of the upper passages, it was far too tight and too awkward to explore, although, like the others, it contained formations that were worthy of attention.

A survey and radio location of this extension were carried out by Haselden, in often wet and freezing conditions. With nothing more sophisticated than a 100ft. fibron tape showing Imperial measurements, he laboriously measured all pitches. A Sunto hand-held compass and a clinometer of the same make also enabled him to complete the survey, and although not a professional surveyor, he was, with the aid of some willing colleagues, able to complete the work in four weeks.

Realising the significance of Crystal Chamber and Pearl Aven, Haselden sought the advice of Frank Baguley, the Hon. Secretary of the Cambrian Caving Council, and Roger Smith, who was the Conservation Officer of the Council and also of the South Wales Caving Club, to see what steps could be taken to preserve the delicate and unique formations found there as, in the case of Pearl Aven, one false step, or even mud falling from a boot, would cause irreparable damage.

An iron grille was placed at the aven's entrance. This not only gives the unique formations the protection they need, but allows visiting cavers to appreciate their beauty without having to come in contact with them. Recommended routes have also been marked off for cavers to follow, and as access into **Crystal Cave** can only be made from Pearl Aven, this cave has also been given protection.

Good caving practice is always essential to preserve delicate formations, and to facilitate this, the Caving Club has recommended that, in the interest of preservation, a maximum of four experienced cavers only can visit these extensions at any given time; a practice which is appreciated and observed by all.

These recently discovered passages were soon found to link up with those beyond Davy Prices's Hall, bringing the total length explored to nearly five miles.

Main Caves:
New Discoveries
Phase II 1964-67

Following the reopening of the caves, at Whitsun, 1964, Dan yr Ogof entered an exciting new era, and by an agreement between the Cave owners and members of The South Wales Caving Club, many outstanding and spectacular discoveries were made and detailed scientific studies were carried out.

The possibility that Dan yr Ogof had more passages to reveal spurred on many of the Club's members who made it their principal objective. There had been no major caving discoveries in Britain for several years, and a new breed of cavers, with improved equipment, was about to break on the South Wales scene, with particular emphasis on Dan yr Ogof.

Caving clubs from other parts of the country also became interested, and as soon as the caves were reopened, Phase II of the explorations, which they were called, was begun under the leadership of the late Alan Coase, who was, at the time, a College Lecturer from Leicestershire. With his companions, he achieved immediate success when considerable extensions to the high series above **Boulder Chamber** were found. From then on, the great push into the mountain to discover new extensions was underway!

In the November, he, along with fellow members, Charles Henson and Doug Baguley, discovered what is called the Syphon Series between Lakes 3 and 4, which were found to be extremely narrow, and muddy. These ultimately extended through the **Mud sump** to reach Lakes 5 and 6.

Later, a solo dive by Charles George, an expert diver, into Lake 6 produced a surprising result when he found himself in a another, much larger lake, No. 7. Despite attempts by him and others who had come from Yorkshire, the Mendips and the Midlands, including a group from Swansea University, no way forward via this route could be found. It was then conceded that, if a breakthrough to the rest of the complex were to be achieved, the notorious 'Tight Squeeze' encountered in 1937 would have to be passed.

The **Endless Crawl,** as it became known, was the likely breakthrough point, but despite many attempts to pass through this 18-inch-high meandering tube, it still remained impassable. It formed a tight double bend at its end, called the Squeeze, that made passing difficult. The passage also posed a great psychological barrier, with cavers fearing, that once inside, they might not be able to turn around.

Efforts were made to widen it with hammer and chisel by a team consisting of Alan Coase, Bruce Foster and Neil Anderson, in company with students from Hickey Grammar School, but still no one could get through.

Undeterred, the South Wales Caving Club mounted another 'push' early in 1966. In the party was 24-year-old Eileen Davies, a domestic science teacher at the Bridgend Technical College. Being of slim build, she had previously taken a look at the Crawl and thought she could get through. Then, on 3rd April, with her ability to squeeze through places too narrow for others, she entered the narrow tube and, ignoring the claustrophobic conditions, she slowly wriggled her way along, to concentrate on the strong draught which was blowing through. She managed to pass the Squeeze but came up against a deep 'chimney' which went vertically downwards to reach what looked like a chamber. In order to get down this shaft, she reported that a ladder was urgently required.

A follow-up visit took place on Easter Tuesday, the 12th April, after the Manager, Mr Trevor Lewis, had satisfied himself that the exceptional amount of rain which had fallen the day before had not flooded the four lakes beyond Bridge Chamber. In the team was the late Bruce Foster, then a 22-year-old student who, being of slim build and one of the Club's smallest

In Flabbergasm Chasm
(Reproduced by kind permission of Mr Tony Baker)

and most agile members, was another ideal candidate for tackling **The Crawl**. Then he, preceded by Miss Davies, began their arduous journey through the 350ft long tube.

Inside, they found conditions extremely 'tight' and had to chip way at the rock for extra room when they found their frogmen's suits getting torn on sharp pieces of projecting rock. Then, after inching their way along for two and a half hours, they finally came to the chimney. To their despair, the ladder they had brought was too short, so Bruce Foster had to negotiate **The Crawl** all over again to get a longer one.

At the end of **The Crawl,** some initials scrawled in the mud told them that people had been that way before, and it was discovered that the initials P. O. belonged to Peter Ogden of The Swansea University Caving Club, who, in company with Terry Moon, had been the first to 'conquer' the dreadful Crawl, and had probably been unable to descend the vertical shaft for lack of the proper equipment.

Once Bruce Foster and company had descended the 'chimney', they found themselves standing inside a large cavern with a waterfall sounding in the darkness. Immediately, they were overwhelmed at finding such a spectacular place and went back to inform their companions. During this time, two members of the team had been sent back to the surface, to check on the weather conditions and to gather a second team to bring along extra food and lights.

Rod Steward, an engineer from Gloucester, and the late Bill Little, who had the distinction of being Chairman of the Cave Research Group of Great Britain, were the other members of the Club who had joined the party, and the five of them followed Miss Davies and Mr Foster through **The Endless Crawl** to descend into the newly discovered cavern which was named **Gerard Platten Hall** in recognition of Mr Platten's contributions to Dan yr Ogof before the war.

There was a small stream flowing across the floor. This eventually led to a massive boulder fall which looked impassable. Downstream, mud banks had formed on either side, and, after a distance of 40m/132ft, the stream fell into a pot or hole in the floor. A later climb down this established that it led to the numerous other caves which made up **The Lower Series.** Across the passage was an arch of pure white calcite and, after a few yards, they came to a lovely crystal pool. This was the start to one of the most breathtaking passages they had yet encountered, filled with magnificent rock formations and columns. The roof, measuring fifty feet high, was vaulted and rose like a Norman arch. They also came across the longest straws they had yet seen, many of them reaching 10 feet. One such straw was so fragile that breathing made it tremble.

Seeing so many breathtaking formations accumulated in one place brought forth gasps of admiration and, as words to describe such an enchanting place failed them, they called it **Flabbergasm Chasm.**

Later, Bruce Foster told reporters: 'We were so excited, we went numb with awe. Finding something like this is what every caver dreams of.'

Ahead was another crystal pool and then, after a long walk of about 90m/300ft, the passage came to an abrupt end with a 7m/25ft overhanging decent into another memorable cavern. This started off as a 3m/9ft high meandering tube, similar in size and characteristics to the one at the beginning of the Show-cave, but it became extremely high and this earned it the name of **Grand Canyon**. It also had a sandy floor. Here, the party realised that they had entered a new world of gigantic proportions and unbelievable natural beauty.

Down one side of **Grand Canyon** were mud banks with some magnificent formations, which included helictites: stalactites growing out sideways. Among their twisted shapes were crystal pools, pearls and 'flowers' created by drips falling on mud, causing this section to be called **The Flower Gardens.** Beyond, the height of **Grand Canyon** decreased to just 6 feet until, at its farthest end, it came down to floor level. Here, they managed to climb up a 2m/6ft mud slope to enter **Monk Hall,** where to their surprise, they found themselves looking at blood-red stalagmites with a grotesquely shaped one hunched like a hooded monk. The Red Monk, as this curious formation was called, stood beneath another stunning display of straws. The red coloured stalactites glimmered in their lights, as did the crystal pool with an ice-like covering of thin, soft, green calcite, thus making this 70-foot-high cavern another spectacular find and another great achievement for the caving team.

From here, two large passages proceeded in different directions but both ended in disappointing boulder falls. In following the one sweeping around to the left, they came to **Cloud Chamber,** so named because of its hundreds of straw stalactites, hanging close together above their heads like an enormous 'white cloud'. Many of these reached 15 feet, the longest in Wales, and were said to make Straw Chamber 'look like a small grotto'. One exceptional straw had actually formed a single column with a stalagmite, and appeared fragile in so large a place.

A small stream was making its way across the cavern, only to disappear down a hole into what they called **Four Pots Passage,** which turned out to be a tortuous connection to the **Lower Series –** where it eventually forms the "Shower" above the entrance to another labyrinth of passages known as **The Mazeways.**

Cloud Chamber also quickly diminished in size, and to the sound of cascading water, just half a mile beyond **Flabbergasm Chasm,** they entered **Cascades Aven.** Here, they were confronted with the astonishing sight of a 100-foot waterfall and a vertical rock barrier. Wondering if the aven led anywhere, they decided to get to the top.

Grasping hold of the rock for foot and hand-holds, climbing the barrier proved difficult but was well worth the effort. After a short distance, they were amazed to see the start of a deep and narrow, green-coloured canal. They also found the entrance to a 45-foot-high cavern they were to call **Hanger Passage.** At its far end they encountered a solid rock fall that looked impassable.

They were later to discover from dye tests that the water from the Cascades originated from Pwll-y-Wydden Fawr on the surface, and that the Cascades disappeared into the bottom of the aven to enter **Thixotropic Passage** in the **Lower Series.**

Entering Cloud Chamber
Alan Coase Collection

On entering **The Green Canal**, an ice-cold swim in the deep water confirmed that the use of a dinghy was more appropriate, and they decided to return with one.

In any event, this epic underground journey had taken almost fifteen hours to accomplish and, weary after their endeavours, the party decided to make their way back to their starting point and finally surfaced with their jubilant news at 3 a.m.

Greeting them in the Restaurant was Dr Alfred Price, father of Mr Ashford Price, and Chairman of Dan yr Ogof, with offers of much needed refreshment.

Also greeting them was a number of journalists who had been waiting anxiously in a snowstorm for what they termed 'the discovery story of the year.'

The discoveries certainly thrilled the people of the Swansea Valley who had waited patiently for news of their progress. Such was the measure of their interest, that Mr Trevor Lewis had also received numerous telephone calls requesting information.

The party was overwhelmed by the interest they had received, and Eileen Davies was proclaimed a heroine.

Because these astounding discoveries were made towards the end of the holiday weekend, many who had made a contribution towards the final success were already back at their jobs. It was also reported, that despite the cold and wet weather, 3,000 people had visited the Show-cave on Easter Monday alone.

Keeping the momentum of their success going, Eileen Davies, along with Bruce Foster, Neil Anderson, Rod Stewart and Charles George, returned on the 14th April with dinghies to cross The Green Canal. After paddling for 200 yards along this three-foot-wide waterway, Eileen Davies and Bruce Foster found they could climb into **Hanger Passage.** Using the other dinghy, they carried out a ferry service, taking the others down the canal to the new cave. As the canal widened, it also became shallower, enabling them to wade safely.

At the end of **The Green Canal,** they entered what they called **Go Faster Passage,** which continued with a sandy floor and ended in **Surprise Chamber.** The route ahead was said to lie to the right, along a narrow slit, just before reaching 'the sand banks'. Then going along **Go Slower Passage,** which started out as a narrow traverse but gradually became larger, they came to a large water-worn cavern which appeared to have no floor. Above the abyss was an aven which accentuated its depth. It was calculated that the distance from the top of the aven to the bottom of the Abyss was 100 feet.

At first, this gaping hole looked impassable, but a passage soon led to another very high but curiously shaped chamber which was 20-30 feet across and had a waterfall cascading down its almost perpendicular wall at the far end. A mass of boulders lay across the floor and led to the cave to be called **Rottenstone Aven.**

Still the discoveries went on! Next came another spacious cavern with deep sandy deposits. They called this cave **Bat Chamber.** Beyond, the section they called **High Way** was much larger, and at its end there was a water-filled tube called a sump. They were unable to enter this, and as it marked the furthermost point they could reach that day, they returned weary but triumphant to the surface.

Again an enthusiastic welcome awaited them, with reporters eager to hear what they had discovered. It was found that another one and a half miles of passages had been discovered. Thus, Dan yr Ogof grew a little more in stature as well as in length.

On the 30th April, another expedition set out to examine **The Abyss,** and this almost perpendicular 'shaft' was bravely descended by a rope ladder. At the bottom was a long winding passage, and because of its muddy condition, with banks of mud kept constantly wet by streams, it was called **Thixotropic Passage.** It seemed to go on interminably into the mountain. Wondering where it was going to lead, they followed its route and came across a deep lake, **Lake 10.** They also encountered deep water at the start of another extremely long passage which was another amazing find. Circular in

Negotiating The Green Canal, 1966
(Reproduced by kind permission of the Observer *Magazine)*

character and 3-4 metres in diameter, it closely resembled the tube on the London Underground and was aptly named **Bakerloo Straight.**

At its far end, the passage divided into two parts. The right hand one was low and called **Worm's Way**; it led directly back to **The Grand Canyon,** thus completing the circuit and providing an alternative way back to Dan yr Ogof I. The next day, the left hand turning from **Bakerloo**

The Lower Series: Bakerloo Straight
(Reproduced by kind permission of Mr Tony Baker)

Straight was explored. This was found to lead back to **Gerard Platten Hall** and was named **Virgin Passage**. Interestingly, some more lakes were found along its route. Heavy snowfalls and subsequent flooding halted further progress for some weeks, although Bruce Foster, with Laurie Gilpin, and Bill Little, managed, in very marginal conditions, to remove the **Squeeze** at the end of **The Endless Crawl** to make travelling through much easier. Then, after an epic free climb down **The Abyss**, another significant find came to light with the discovery of some curiously-shaped formations which made another spectacular display of great beauty and variety. Called **Dali's Delight,** the formations were considered similar to the images which the artist Salvadore Dali presented on canvas.

Following the recent finds, the South Wales Caving Club decided that serious thought should be given to cave science; and since there was a need to carry out a scientific study on cave life, The Caving Club, backed by the Cave Management, imposed a voluntary ban on further exploration so that the work could be carried out effectively and without risking further pollution to the fragile environment. This break was also used to photograph the various formations.

Survey of the caves was carried out using a 'survey unit' which consisted of a liquid-filled prismatic compass of the Army marching type, mounted on two ex army tripods, one of them cut down to suit the smaller passages, and a 3-metre-long hinged staff for sighting on to and for taking height and cross measurements in the larger passages. A 30 metre "Fibron" tape was used for all centre line measurements. Radio magnetic location checks were made at a number of points for both position and depth. Some passages were surveyed using a hand-held 'Sunto' compass, and a clinometer for measuring slopes.

Aerial photographs of Dan yr Ogof's catchment area on the surface showed the locations of the various sink holes – places where streams disappear into the mountain.

Bat Chamber, situated one and a half miles from the entrance, was selected as the best place to carry out this scientific study because of its dry sandy floor, and, under the leadership of Alan Coase, a team of seven men and Eileen Inson, née Davies, set up camp there in the May, 1966. In addition to the usual camping gear they took along enough drinking water and food to enable them to remain there for as long as was necessary. They also took along a field telephone to keep in touch with the surface. Whilst below, they quickly learned that it was not as cold in the cave as was first thought. It remained at a constant 48° F throughout their stay, thus enabling them to spend more time studying life forms and gathering soil for analysis.

After spending nearly a week underground, the party surfaced with a mass of scientific data which would help to determine the origin of the cave system. The data was also required for the preparation of a report to present to interested bodies who might be willing to finance the setting up of an underground laboratory for future studies.

An interesting fact emerged when they surfaced. Members confessed that the longer they had remained underground, the less they wanted to eat. The team had been able to keep to regular meals, starting with a hearty breakfast, a snack at midday, and a three-course evening meal after they had completed the day's work. Although they had been working for long hours, they soon found their appetites dwindling, and much of their food had not been eaten.

This expedition had also generated a great deal of interest on the surface, with Mr Lewis again receiving many hundreds of telephone calls requesting information.

During this time, green fluorescent dye was put into the streams on the surface to see how long it took for the water to travel through the cave system. The main stream of the River Giedd goes underground some two miles away, with a secondary entrance or sink about 1½ miles away. Dye placed in the main Geidd sink, in moderate flood conditions, took 50 hours to reach the resurgence (River Cave) at Dan yr Ogof, thus suggesting that there could be at least ten miles of passages to be discovered in that section. Dye was also put into Waun Fignen Felen, Pwll Dwfn and Pwll-y-Wydden, on the surface also reached the resurgence, giving the cavers a better idea as to the length of time the caves took to flood.

When the test had been made from Sink-y-Geidd, the point of entry to the chosen cave could not be observed, as the low passage leading into the Third Lake had flooded to the roof.

At one time, a 90-foot shaft had been blasted into the mountain top, one and a half miles from the show cave entrance. Water which had gathered in the shaft had also found it way into the caves.

In conditions of extreme flooding, water is forced through a number of fissures around **The Parting of the Ways.** In the past this has been responsible for allowing vast deposits of sand to accumulate here to a depth of 2-3 feet, but the placing of a conduit in the floor now prevents water from entering and has removed the necessity for the continuous removal of the sand, which had been the case after every flood.

Another interesting fact emerged when in an item in *The Evening Post* revealed that, whilst a party were investigating a scree slope, they found snails and dead flies amongst the rubble. This made them think that they were close to the surface, and when a radio location device on the mountain top was successful in pinpointing the party, a ten foot shaft was then dug to reach them.

It was decided by the Management that when exploration re-commenced, special care and precautions would have to be taken to combat the danger of exhaustion with cavers walking greater distances to the newly discovered caves, including the problems associated with the lakes when flooded. Accordingly, to minimise the risk of accidents, The South Wales Caving Club put into operation a 'guest leader' system, whereby only experienced cavers were chosen to take parties into the caves beyond **The Crawl.**

Several visits were made over the winter period of 66/67, but no major extensions were found until the March of 1967, when three major discoveries were made. The first was made by Mrs Eileen Inson. She, accompanied by Colin Fairburn, took a closer look at the boulder pile-up in **Hanger Passage,** and, on the 19th March, they succeeded in going through the blockage to discover a large extension which they called **Hanger South.** To their disappointment, it ended in a large sandy choke.

Another party of four men from The South Wales Caving Club, and a female member, Susan Bradshaw, went in on the 20th, to discover **Hanger North,** but they, too, could make no progress owing to a very unstable choke. Whilst there, they discovered that the small stream in **Hanger Chamber** had found its way into the cavern. These two chambers were comparable in size to their lofty neighbours, a fact borne out by the names they were given.

The third discovery was made by a group of Yorkshire and Lancashire cavers led by David Judson from The South Wales Caving Club, who, on returning from the last choke, found their way into another cavern of enormous proportions, measuring 100 feet wide and 50 feet high. Having climbed 30-40 feet, to near roof level, they were confronted with multicoloured straws which quivered as they passed and which formed a dividing curtain between them and yet another large cavern. This fabulous discovery was called **Quivering Straw Passage.** A hundred yards further on, the group found themselves facing another solid and final boulder fall. Despite this, they found that the so-called **Right Hand Series** led for about 150 yards through several low sandy chambers until, in the end, the way ahead was far too small for them to follow.

Finding new caves was not without its hazards. On one occasion, a female caver fell and broke her leg. A rescue attempt was mounted, but owing to the high level of the water, which prevented her being brought to the surface, the Fire Brigade had to be called to pump it away. There was, unfortunately, a fatality during the early days; a young caver drowned and, despite repeated attempts to find him, his body was never recovered. Another exploration nearly ended in disaster when, in the continuing attempt to find a bypass to the **Endless Crawl,** a fall of sand and boulders completely buried one man. Miraculously, he was pulled out alive.

During the next round of explorations, many new finds were made, but the most significant was the discovery of a way into the section known as **Dan yr Ogof III**, that heralded yet another eventful chapter in the cave's history.

Main Caves: Further Discoveries Phase III

This major new stage in the exploration of Dan yr Ogof was greatly assisted by improvements in the development of caving equipment such as lighter ladders and improved lighting. It was to the cavers' advantage, that with the development of specialised descending and ascending gear, any pitch was rendered possible, of which there were many to negotiate; but the prospect of finding something new as a result of the effort taken was always considered worthwhile. The explorers had also been given a sounder knowledge of their surroundings from the various surveys that had been carried out.

From these surveys, the cavers had also found that all the passages beyond **The Endless Crawl** continued in a south-easterly direction, whilst those from **The Rising** at the end of **High Way,** suddenly turned north.

In September, 1967, as weather conditions were excellent and the water in the lakes was low, enabling them to be crossed, Alan Coase and Terry Moon led in separate parties which included members of the Wessex Caving Club to tackle **The Rising** by trying to reduce the water. This was not successful, but they did manage to scale the 90ft climb immediately above it. This feat took over two hours to accomplish and eventually led them into a small, well-scalloped tube called **Windy Way,** which was said to have three times the draught found in the **Endless Crawl.** Climbing into **Windy Way** was, apparently, a high spirited affair with spontaneous outbreaks of singing and whistling. After crawling on hands and knees for a distance of 150 feet, a steep-sided rift was reached. Using a pitch ladder, they descended this 45 degree traverse and found themselves inside a beautifully decorated passage, its walls covered with some fine helictites ; which must have come as a pleasant interlude after such an arduous crawl. It was Alan Coase's birthday, so this discovery was called **Birthday Passage.** They also found a deep hole through which they could look down on a stream flowing over rippled sand banks some 50 feet below, but, being short on tackle and time, they had to return to the surface.

Intrigued by what they had found, Alan Coase and several other members returned the next day, Sunday, the 25th September. It was reported that the decent of the pitch was 'exhilarating'. Upstream, they found that the roof rose to well over 60 feet, whilst downstream, it came down to a low bedding plane, with the water disappearing between the two slabs of rock. One member, though, managed to squeeze through and found a small lake.

Moving upstream was relatively easy and, as the passage remained high and wide, they made good progress, but after a few hundred yards, boulder piles made walking much more difficult. In between the rock falls, they said, 'There were often several hundred yards of superb sand and gravel-floored open streamway.' They managed to pass a few obstacles quite easily, but as the route continued northwards, the rock falls became more difficult to pass. They decided to halt at what appeared to be a collapsed two-level confluence. This area was also filled with fine sand, in places as much as 20 feet deep and curiously patterned with what were described as 'sand-castles'.

Calcite Formations were more common along this rambling passage, called **High Way Two** or **The Great North Road**, but as it proceeded northwards, the route became extremely hazardous, with piles of fallen rock littering their path. They also found themselves constantly walking in and out of water.

The route went relentlessly on. Nevertheless, they saw some astonishing sights along the way, reporting that they had seen huge slabs of rock which had broken free of the roof, lying in their path, whilst others, not entirely free, were hanging precariously above their heads.

Further along, where the roof rose again, a short climb brought them into a straight-sided chamber, over 30 feet wide and 65 feet high, with a single pinnacle of rock having become detached from the cave wall, standing on its own and leaning over to one side. It was a strange looking feature, wide at the bottom and rising almost to a point. To the right of this **Pinnacle Chamber,** a narrow, vertical tube led to upper passages. Above them, two parallel Avens were found, and when scaled, they reached an even higher level of passages with spectacular 'balconies' overlooking the stream some 100-150 feet below. Then they made another unusual and interesting find. Stretching across a passage was a perfect example of a false floor, created when a stream had left behind a thin crust of stalactite after washing away the glacial fill. Owing to an area of complicated avens and shafts, further progress was halted.

On their return, they went through a high level ox-bow which had a breathtaking display of multicoloured crystal pools. There were also overgrown gour pools and mud flowers across the floor with calcite flowers and more crystals around a dried out pool. 'Cascades' of pure white calcite, suspended from ledges, and some curtains, said to be 'the finest in the system', completed the picture. Superlatives adequate to describe such a thrilling display failed the beholders. They finally decided on calling this remarkable cave **The Mostest.** After a long day underground, such a spectacle must have been an inspiring sight. Even at this great distance into the mountain, Mother Nature had managed to produce this cavern like a well played ace! Further along, they again found their way hampered by piles of boulders and sand which they nicknamed **Blackpool Sands.** At this point, they made a hurried return to the surface, delighted, that at the end of their efforts, their journey had taken them four miles beyond the entrance.

Further exploration was limited and, during the winter of 67/68, other essential work was carried out within the caves, including the widening of the tight bends of **The Endless Crawl** to accommodate taking a rigid stretcher through, as well as establishing an emergency telephone link, and taking in stocks of food which was then stored in the dry passages

Crossing the Lakes
Alan Coase Collection

Pinnacle Chamber
(Reproduced by kind permission of Andy Freem)

The Far North: At the Choke. The End of the Road
(Reproduced by kind permission of Andy Freem)

immediately beyond **The Crawl.** During one such expedition, a half a ton of food and equipment had been carried in.

Later, a party from Yorkshire, led by David Judson, set up camp to spend two full days in **The Great North Road,** described as a stream passage and of 'impressive proportions'. During this time, they went on to reach one of the largest sections found and called the **Great Hall.** They were, however, disappointed to find their path blocked by a pile of boulders that stretched from floor to ceiling, thus giving rise to the fear that they had reached the furthermost point of Dan yr Ogof. They called it **The Far North.**

Very little progress could be made here, partly due to the high water levels in the lakes, and partly because the equipment which was required to continue with the exploration could not be taken through **The Endless Crawl,** even though the passage had been widened. However, there was a determination among the members of The South Wales Caving Club that there had be a way through the various chokes and boulder falls to reach passages that were waiting to be discovered.

With better equipment, Dave Edwards and David Judson successfully scaled the massive blockage in **Rottenstone Aven** and found another interesting chamber, containing magnificent-looking helictites along with blue and green tinted argonite and gypsum formations. Apart from a small and inaccessible passage from which a small stream entered at the top of another aven in the area, the indications were that there was no way forward from there. However, one significant find did emerge during a trip to the **Far North.** Fluorescent green dye placed in Sinc-y-Geidd on the surface was found there by members of the Leeds University Club. They also took an extra look at the passages known as the **Pinnacle Series,** above **Pinnacle Chamber.**

After the three trips in March 1970, something like 450 metres of new passages had been added to the existing 350 already found, which meant that nearly a mile of new passages had been found. These were then surveyed to a very high grade.

The search for new passages went on. Whilst checking the water levels with Alan Coase and two others, Terry Moon found an entrance into an extensive network of passages at the extreme south-easterly end of Dan yr Ogof, called **The Mazeways,** which led into several sumps.

A dry route into what is believed to be the hidden passages of Dan yr Ogof, (DY0 IV) eluded them, and their attention was then centred on the water-filled passages which they hoped would lead into the unexplored section. As diving equipment had also become greatly improved from compressed air to back-mounted cylinders, divers were able to go deeper than the 30 feet maximum allowed by the oxygen breathing apparatus of the 1950s. During diving, one water-filled passage was found to connect with Lake Three and the river beyond.

On 7th October, 1970, another assault was launched on the sumps, but little success was achieved on the main stream owing to heavily silted passages and nil visibility.

Martyn Farr, one of the country's expert cave divers, was the first into **Mazeways One,** but swimming along the underwater passages was a hazardous operation. During one dive, a large chamber, 45 feet in diameter, was discovered, but as this also led nowhere, the dive was discontinued. It was clear that there was no short or easy dive through **Mazeways** which was thought to be the main flood overflow channel for the main stream. Successive dives by Terry Moon, M. Coburn and C. Fairburn also proved unsuccessful, either because the water had became murky, the passages too narrow, or they had ended in an impassable choke. On another occasion, the **Mazeways** Entrance Pool was entered, and the only way forward was via a small tube heading upstream. This eventually terminated in Lake 10.

This lake was dived by Terry Moon and Martyn Farr, but as visibility was virtually nil, no progress was made. Lake 11 was also dived to a depth of over 30 feet in nil visibility, although, immediately above the lake, a high level extension could be seen. This extension was named **Mazeways II**. It is interesting to note, that following the dye tests, the water presumed to come from Sinc-y-Geidd was first seen in **Mazeways II**.

A little later, the sump located in **Dali's Delight** was found to be a back entrance into this complex and was linked with the furthermost point reached in the Deep Sump which was almost double the depth of that found along the normal route from **Mazeways I**.

Disappointment soon followed when subsequent efforts failed to produce any results. It had been hoped to make a connection between Lakes 4 and 8 which, it was said, would effectively reduce the number of porterage required to take in essential equipment, but dives from Lakes 7 and 8 soon quashed this idea when the route was found to be over 50 feet deep and beset with obstacles.

On 30th July, 1972, some success was achieved when a dive in **Mazeways II** produced 300 metres of passages which meant that, little by little, the Black Mountain had begun to yield to the dogged determination of the Cave divers. Although they were able to progress a great distance along the water filled passages, often in dangerous conditions, the prospect of finding a way into what was called the **Geidd Series** still eluded them.

In spite of this disappointment, The South Wales Caving Club continued to probe into the system and, in the August of 1978, a party of ten cavers led by Gareth Davies from Abercrave and John Bowden, an airline employee at Gatwick Airport, set up a six-day camp to carry out further exploration based on Alan Coase's theories on where the extra passages might be found. About 500 feet below the surface and 4 miles in from the Show-cave, they succeeded in finding three new passages, the longest of which was 1,000 feet long, 15 feet wide and 40 feet high which were said to give tremendous scope for future explorations.

For such a trip, each man carried 80 1bs. of equipment. Their diet consisted of dehydrated food, mainly rice, dried vegetables, orange drinks and peanuts. They also carried out some underwater exploration and, on arriving back, they found as their suits had been immersed so long in water, that they were coming apart at the seams and that their elbows and knees were showing through the neoprene.

They reported that some of their most hazardous moments had come when they were traversing sand ledges which could have given way at any moment. Another danger was in negotiating a very unstable boulder choke when several hundredweight of stones were liable to fall as each man passed through. Although they were aware of the dangers, they had, nevertheless, overcome them.

On surfacing, Gareth Davies commented: 'We have achieved all that we wanted to. We had four or five projects going at the same time, and are delighted at the prospects we have uncovered for future sorties into the caves.' He also stated: 'The feeling of teamwork was unbelievable. The whole project involved a tremendous amount of brute force and we really had to grit our teeth in carrying all that stuff, but we sorted ourselves out once we got there.'

The team also reported that they did not require the use of tents. Most of them had sleeping bags made of synthetic material to keep them warm, and although they had donned three or four layers of clothing to maintain their body temperatures, they found that putting on cold, and often damp, wet suits upon waking was their worst experience.

On surfacing, as well as passing lines of curious visitors, they were officially greeted by the directors of the Company, including Mr Ashford Price, the Development Director, who acknowledged the importance of such a survey.

In 1982, another probe into the **Great North Road** was undertaken by Tony Knibbs, Roger Wittington and Martin Rowe. A quick reconnaissance took them into North Aven and the upper end of **The Mostest** but, after a while, Martin Rowe's lamp failed. Roger Wittington went on to climb 50 feet up North Aven and reached Overpass Passage, which bypassed the difficult section. There was, he said, 'an atmosphere of complete remoteness about the place,' which increased as they progressed towards the massive Choke itself. With their footsteps deadened by the sand drifts, no sound could be heard, and the 'profound silence' they described 'greatly accentuated the remoteness of the area'.

On their return, an hour and a half later, they found that an overnight fall of rain had swelled the lakes and had made the waterfalls 'sound even louder'. They finally emerged into the daylight via the River Cave.

Of his experience, Tony Knibbs wrote: 'For me, the trip was the fulfilment of thirty years of caving. With caves like Dan yr Ogof, it is hardly surprising that a mild attack of carboniferous curiosity should turn into such a chronic, enjoyable, incurable and hilarious ailment.'

In their continuing search for the missing passages, a meeting with The South Wales Caving Club at *The Copper Beech* in Abercrave, decided to use a number of modern techniques as part of their investigations. Satellite pictures and infra-red photographs were to be used to detect the differences in the rock. Advanced radio techniques were also to be used to track the extent of the hidden passages with the caver transmitting to someone on the surface, who would then continue to monitor the signals showing the density of the rock and the path of any hollow passages. Botanists, too, were to lend a hand by analysing the plants on the surface above the caves. From their examination of the grasses and mosses, they hoped to tell what lay beneath the soil.

In 1998, mining engineers from Tower Colliery, Hirwaun, were recruited to help with the search, and began drilling bore-holes into the limestone ceilings of caverns where geologists thought the hidden 10 miles of passages were likely to be. Having successfully discovered a cave immediately above one, although seemingly filled with mud, the Management placed a wheelbarrow beneath to catch the mud trickling through. Such was the volume, that in the morning, they found that the wheelbarrow had been completely submerged by the deluge which had poured through.

Thrilled by the fact that there was evidence of missing passages above and just where the geologists had said they would be, it was now the hope of Mr Ashford Price, that a way in could be found to reveal even more spectacular finds which have remained hidden for millions of years.

Martyn Farr went to examine the new cave and found it very cramped. It only allowed him to kneel. Who knows? This cave could well lead on to others, and then Dan yr Ogof would really open out to yet another fascinating and spectacular phase.

The end of the Twentieth Century saw the completion of sixty glorious years in the history of Dan yr Ogof and of caving in South Wales, which, in true Dan yr Ogof style, ended on an encouraging note with a hint of spectacular things to follow.

Never before in Wales had there been such an extreme effort to explore a system to the full. The enthusiasm and devotion displayed by individual cavers has been commendable. Without such a concerted effort, none of Dan yr Ogof's amazing caverns would have been found.

Meanwhile, other attractions were being developed in the complex to ensure that everyone has an enjoyable time.

Bone Cave: Further Discoveries 1978

Taking time off from their caving activities in the main show-cave, members of The South Wales Caving Club, and various helpers, re-commenced excavations in the **Bone Cave** which began with clearance of the remaining boulder obstacles in preparation for Mr Edmund 'Ted' Mason, who returned with his wife and several others, in March, 1978, to search for relics which might have fallen in between the boulders and had become lost. With the assistance of lights attached to their helmets, close scrutiny of the cleared floor soon produced a bronze object shaped like an egg cup.

They also found the skull of a young woman which had become partly embedded in a dome of stalagmite that had formed since Roman times. The woman was said to have lived in the 2nd Century. The neck bones of a young woman were also found which could have become separated from the skull. Close by were the larger bones of a man.

Mr Mason returned again in the October, to spend an entire weekend, 'to find out more about the people who had lived there', and succeeded in discovering eight more Roman coins, dated to the 4th Century. These are now in the possession of The National Museum of Wales in Cardiff. Mr Edward Besley, Numismatist, in charge of the Roman coins at the Department of Archaeology at The National Museum, arranged for a selection of the coins discovered in the cave to be photographed and, going in a clockwise direction, has identified them as follows:- Top centre:

1. Bronze *nummus* showing the head of Constantius II, the son of

Constantine I, who was Emperor at the time: AD 324-337. The coin was minted at Trier in the Moselle Region of Germany, which became a commercial and cultural centre under the Romans. This coin also bears the head of Constantine's son;

2. Bronze *nummus* with the wording '*Urbs Roma*'. This was a commemorative issue and minted at Trier.

3. Bronze *nummus* (obverse) with the wording '*Constantinopolis*' around the outside edge, to mark the fact that Constantine I had moved his capital from Rome to Constantinople. This was a commemorative issue and also minted at Trier.

4. Bronze *nummus* of Constantius II (reverse) showing two soldiers, each holding a standard. Minted at Lyon, France.

5. Bronze *nummus* (reverse). Marked *Constantinopolis,* with the winged figure of Victory standing on a prow. Minted at Trier;

6. Silver *denarius* showing the head of Emperor Vespasian, AD 69-79. Minted in Rome.

7. Centre Coin: Brass *sesterius*, showing the head of Hadrian, AD 117-138. Minted in Rome. Dark brown in colour.

Apart from the silver *denarius*, the bronze coins had all discoloured with age. The most significant find, though, came from the area marked O/n, when a large 'Dolphin' brooch, dated to the 1st Century, surfaced.

This fine specimen was much larger than the one found in 1938, being 89 mm long and weighing almost 60g. It had an iron pin on a bronze spindle and was finely decorated. A rare feature was the pierced catchplate.

Brooches of this type were fairly common in Britain and first came into existence around AD 50, soon after the Roman conquest. It was obvious from the rubbing found on the metal, that it had been well worn. The brooch was similar in characteristics to the one found in Caerwent, and now in the Newport Museum. This particular brooch is on display with the rest of the Roman jewellery at The National Museum of Wales.

As no other items were found, Mr Mason had reason to believe that

A collection of the Roman Coins found in the Cave
(Reproduced by kind permission of The National Museums and Galleries of Wales)

the cave had relinquished all its treasures, thus making it available for opening to the public. To make it possible for the public to reach the cave with ease, a flight of concrete steps was built at the far end of the Dinosaur Park, from the top of which one can look back on the rest of the Complex. From this elevated position, the visitor can stop to admire the splendid panorama of the locality with the Brecon Beacons beyond. The full measure of their beauty is realised at a glance with only the sound of distant traffic spasmodically breaking the peaceful tranquillity of the area. In summer, too, the smooth contours of the Beacons are the colour of sand and form a contrast to the green wooded slopes across the way.

From here, too, the visitor can look down on the dinosaur park, where the models of the creatures appear no larger than toys. The tops of the Coffee Shop, Museum and Ticket Office can also be seen appearing above the trees.

Ahead of the steps is the covered walkway which takes the visitor up the cliff face. For the gradual climb, hard hats have to be worn to protect banging one's head against the roof of the canopy. The hats, which fit all head sizes, are collected at the bottom of the path.

At the top of the walkway, a covered bridge extends across the steep gorge to take the visitor directly into the cave. From here, too, there is a glorious view of the valley. The four-foot-high entrance and tunnel have been substantially enlarged to enable us all to enter without stooping.

With the help of archaeologists from the University College of Wales and The National Museum in Cardiff, the cave was opened in March 1979, for an exhibition with 'The history of man's existence and dependency on caves' as the chosen theme. This exhibition included several tableaux depicting life in prehistoric times with a taped commentary given by Dr Anne Eddington of University College.

The exhibition was an instant success and the cave was proclaimed Europe's first Archaeological Interpretative Centre for explaining history, for which Mr Ashford Price received an Award at a ceremony in Cardiff Castle.

Then, on the 10th April, 1985, the cave was officially opened to the general public by Lord Parry of Neyland, then Chairman of the Welsh Tourist Board, who, after being given a conducted tour of the main Show Cave, was entertained to a lunch inside the magnificent surroundings of the Cathedral Cave.

Upon entering The Bone Cave, the present day visitor is immediately aware of its compactness, made more so by the installation of the high wired screen which the Management were obliged to install, to prevent vandals and 'souvenir hunters' from damaging the formations, as had been the unfortunate case in the main Show-Cave.

On looking upwards, attention is drawn to the curious patterns made by the moonmilk stretching across the ceiling, but the most spectacular formation is that of the large spongy mass which has erupted down the eastern wall and was noted by the 1923 archaeologists.

The tableaux which related to prehistoric burial scenes have since been moved to the Cathedral Cave, and include the colourful effigy of the Roman Legionnaire who stood in full regalia just inside the entrance.

The reconstruction of the 1938 archaeological dig has been left in place and still provides a colourful picture of how the archaeologists worked in the cramped conditions and illustrates what equipment they used. A couple of human skulls placed amongst the workings remind the visitor of the spectacular discoveries that were made there.

However, the visitors' attention is drawn to a tableau showing a family roasting a deer. Nearby is a weaving loom, as would have been used for making clothes, and amongst the various cooking pots, is a shield and other weapons used at that time. In the far corner of the cave are scenes showing the different animals, such as the bear, sabre toothed tiger, hyena and wolf, which lived in caves during prehistoric times. Another taped commentary to suit the displays explains the history of the age, with special lighting effects to create a realistic atmosphere that transports the visitor back in time.

The cave has also been judged to be among the top twenty tourist attractions in Britain in explaining history, and with some 200,000 visitors coming each year, the cave is now equal in popularity to Madame Taussaud's, in London. Some 145,000 school children come each year to learn how caves were created and about the people who lived in them, thus combining geology with a history lesson on man's early existence.

When it was thought that the cave had revealed all its secrets, Mr Ashford Price, whilst carrying out a routine check of the cave one night with his golden haired Labrador, found himself being presented with a human bone the archaeologists had left behind after the dog went sniffing in a corner, and this led to other bones being found. The bones from the Bronze Age were then put on display before being taken away for examination.

Then, as late as 1980, whilst fixing a light cable, Mr Price came across a 3,000-year-old skull of a child which had been lying all those years within a few inches of thousands of passing feet. The skull was said to have been the best they had discovered and, despite its great age, all the teeth were in 'perfect condition'. It, too, was sent off to University College for examination.

In 1991, a rare Roman artefact was the next item to come to light when workmen came across a sandstone measuring six-and-a-half inches long and four-and-a-half inches wide. Thinking it had some historic significance, the workmen handed it over for examination and it was identified as a stone on which Roman soldiers sharpened their weapons. The sandstone was in perfect condition and had been shaped so that it could be used from whatever angle it was held. 'Someone must have sat down for hours to get the right shape,' commented the present Manager, Mr Ian Gwilym, to a journalist who was reporting the matter for *The Evening Post*.

Then, a year later, whilst patrolling the cave with Mr Price's son, James, Jenny, the family's Labrador, found a human thigh bone from the Bronze Age. Jenny, with an obvious liking for bones, had become expert in unearthing those the archaeologists had left behind and, therefore, it was added to the amazing total of three thousand already found.

The cave, with its special magic, continues to attract us up the cliff face, just as it had drawn the people who found refuge there. We might never learn who the dwellers actually were, but by leaving behind such a wealth of objects, they have given us an excellent insight into an age about which we would otherwise have known very little.

The excavations inside Yr Ogof have certainly provided us with a clearer picture of how our earliest ancestors lived.

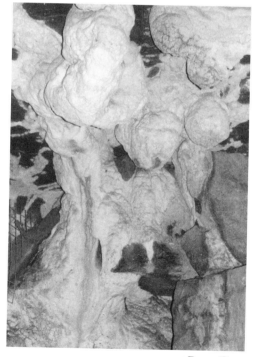

Bone Cave
Formation down Eastern Wall

Outside Attractions:
Iron Age Village

With land to spare in the Complex, the idea of creating outside attractions became a pleasing prospect and the hillside immediately behind the Souvenir Shop and Museum became an excellent site for the construction of an Iron Age Farm.

The inhabitants of the farm would have found that the area provided them with a good living, providing them with both materials to build their homes and food to feed themselves. There was an abundance of water, with a steady supply of fish from the river Tawe, and the land would have provided them with a plentiful supply of rabbits, and fresh fruit at the end of each summer, when blackberries grow in abundance. Farmyard animals such as pigs would also have been kept to provide meat, and there would have been chickens for both meat and eggs. To protect themselves from attack, a boundary fence was built and made of strong, sharp-ended stakes for greater protection.

The reconstruction of the Iron Age Village on the site is a half scale model of what a typical Iron Age farmstead would have looked like. In the reconstruction we see:

1. Chicken Hut
2. A partially constructed hut.
3. A corn store with flat stones on top of a main wooden structure. This was to keep rodents out of the corn area.
4. A look-out point – usually built at the highest point of the village, so as to see an approaching enemy.

Model Of Iron Age Village

5. Haystack used for winter feed for the animals.
6. A storage shed.
7. The main hut.

The Iron Age chimney-shaped furnace shown is the most likely design to have been used to smelt iron ore. It was made primarily of clay over a hazel framework, and had a hole at the top through which the heat and steam escaped.

Iron ore, charcoal and limestone were used. When the furnace had reached a sufficient temperature to melt out the iron, the liquid would then run through the grid and clinker at the bottom and collect into a ball-shaped lump of pig iron. It would then be taken away to the Smithy to have the impurities hammered out before being manufactured into tools or weapons, etc.

Domestic items were made of wood, and food was eaten off wooden platters. Beer was also brewed, and was drunk on festive occasions. Pits were dug for the storage of green crops to use as winter animal feed, and hay-making in the summer was a major event, with some of the hay used as a floor covering, or to stuff mattresses for sleeping.

With an abundance of sheep in the area, wool was readily available for weaving, and combs made of bone became ideal implements for preparing the wool for spinning. Looms would have been easy to construct and a replica of one can be seen in The National Museum of Wales.

It is interesting to note that aerial photographs have shown that farming took place at Dan yr Ogof at the time of the Iron Age (700 years BC – AD 75).

Passing the Farm, the path leads the visitor up to the **Dinosaur Park,** now the largest in Northern Europe, and the entrance is located at the top of the **Geological Trail,** just before it divides to take the visitor on to the Cathedral Cave.

Dinosaur Park

The side of the mountain above the entrance to the Show-cave was levelled and then landscaped to create a wonderland of entertainment for Dan yr Ogof's youngest visitors, and to show them the massive creatures that roamed this earth millions of years ago. This has been achieved with an impressive collection of life-sized models.

An attractive feature of the Dinosaur Park is the water cascade which provides a natural setting for the many smaller dinosaurs. This feature also allows the visitor to view the creatures at close quarters whilst walking up the adjoining steps to the Bone Cave. In the centre of the Park is a pool with an interesting group of dinosaurs which lived in water. These include the crocodile-like **Tylorsaurus,** with a line of spikes extending down the centre of its back to the tip of its tail; the long-necked **Elasmorsaurus,** and the **Tanysatopheus,** whose long snake-like neck makes it a ferocious looking creature. Then, on a bank on the other side of the boundary fence, is a scene from the Pleistocene Period (Ice Age), when animals drank from small ponds which were often rimmed with a sticky mass of asphalt. The scene depicts an archaic elephant that has become trapped in the sticky substance and is at the mercy of a smilodon or sabre toothed tiger, which, in attacking the elephant, has also become trapped. Such occurrences often resulted in the death of both animals.

Usually, older smilodons realised the danger and kept away from the ponds, but many skeletons of young ones have been found, who probably died after they had been lured to the pitch ponds by the prospect of an easy meal. The Park also functions as a pleasant resting area for those wishing to take stock of the glorious surroundings and enjoy the relaxing ambience of the place. It is also safe for the children to run around and see the models at close quarters and to get their parents to photograph them with their favourite one.

The models of the dinosaurs are not only confined to the Park. Many are situated on various sites around the Complex. The first dinosaur the visitor sees on going through the turnstiles, is the horned **Torosaurus,** which was the largest of the frilled Centopasians – the name given to the plant-eating dinosaurs with horns. It had the largest head of any known land animal (over 8 feet/2.6m) It was probably capable of resisting attack from the largest of its contemporary predators, with its horn, no doubt, playing a large part in its defence. It was also the last of the dinosaurs to have lived in the latter part of the Cretaceous Period (180-70 millions years ago).

Behind is the long-necked, plant-eating **Brachiosaurus.** These dinosaurs were 74 feet/22.5m long and weighed approximately 80 tonnes. Brachiosaurus belonged to the Sauropods, and fossil footprints found in America have indicated that they were herding animals who looked after their young.

Then, there is the fierce looking **Allosaurus,** whose aggressive stance sends out a challenge to those of us entering the Coffee Shop. A thick, short neck supported their massive heads. They also had massive feet and three large fingers with long talons which, with their strong jaws, were able to tear their victims apart. They lived in Upper Jurassic Times and their remains have been found in western America.

There are also some very impressive looking models to see amongst the trees whilst walking up the Geological Trail to the Cathedral Cave. They include:

Chasmosauruskaiseni: This dinosaur was 16 feet/5.2m long and had a bony frill at the back of the skull, which was longer than the head itself. The frill had large openings in its bony structure which were probably filled with muscle and covered with skin. The square-shaped frill was lined with small pointed bones. It also had a short horn and long, pointed eyebrow horns. It was thought that these creatures discouraged attacks by swinging their heads from side to side.

Close by is the peculiar looking **Anatosaurus,** whose mouth is shaped like a duck's bill. Another oddity of this dinosaur is, that whilst it has five front toes, it only has three at the back, albeit much larger ones. It is hard to believe that this creature had as many as five hundred teeth in each of its jaws.

Muttaburassurus: This curious looking dinosaur came from Australia and lived during the Cretaceous Times. It was about 23 feet long and had a broad head with a bony lump above its snout. It was thought that their teeth were used for chopping up plants.

Parasaurophus: This breed lived on vegetation which they were able to gnash with their powerful jaws. They also had long crests on top of their heads in which were hollow tubes connected to their throats, thus enabling them to make a bellowing or hooting sound which was crucial when warning others of impending danger. They had long tails which acted as counter balances when they stood on their hind legs. The females of the species had less spectacular crests than the males.

Spinosaurus: This dinosaur grew up to 33-39 feet/10-12m and had a 6 foot/1.8m dorsal fin on its back. This appeared to act as a support for the long sail of skin, which, it is thought, was able to keep its body cool during the hot Cretaceous Period, in Africa.

Corythosaurus: The crest on top of its head resembled a large disc and probably contained tubes which enabled it to make a sound. These creatures grew up to 33 feet/19m high and were the last of the dinosaurs to become extinct.

Pachycephalosaurus: This dinosaur was a plant-eater, weighed one or two tonnes and lived 64 million years ago, during the end of the Cretaceous Period.

It grew up to 26 feet/8m long and had massively thick skull bones that gave its head a dome-like appearance. The thickened skull bones acted like a crash helmet when the dinosaurs butted each other; believed to be a ritual for fighting off a rival during mating – as depicted by the models seen at the back of the trees.

Mamenchisaurus: This dinosaur was a plant-eating Sauropod and lived about 145 million years ago, during the Late Jurassic Period, and is featured with its offspring. They had massive long necks, 33 feet/10 m long, which were just under half of their total length of 72 feet. Their sheer size rendered them immune from attack. If they were, a large claw on the inner toe of each foot was used as a defensive weapon. Like all Sauropods, it went around in herds and protected its young from attack by keeping them in the centre of the group. When these dinosaurs stood on their hind legs, their tails would act as counterbalances. Their remains have been found in China.

Deinoschus: This ferocious looking beast dominates the top of the Trail. With an overall length of 40-50 feet, it was the largest crocodile ever found, was aptly called 'the terrible crocodile', and came from the Rio Grande, in Texas. It was a typical amphibian which occasionally preyed upon unsuspecting sauropods.

Another favourite is the **Mammoth** which can be seen outside the exit door of the Museum. This large, hairy animal, ancestor of the present day elephant, was probably Siberian in origin, and its remains have been found all over Europe. The Mammoth eventually spread to North America via North Asia when the land was joined together. It lived off twigs from various coniferous trees as well as willows, birches and elms. Its trunk was probably used to lower tree branches that were too high, or to scrape away the snow to get to the vegetation beneath. Mammoths were slaughtered in great numbers by Man, for food, during the Pleistocene Period, and many completely preserved carcasses have been discovered in some glacial regions of the Continent.

Evidence that dinosaurs once existed first came to light in the Netherlands in 1780, when a skull of one was found in a chalk quarry in

Maastricht. As it looked like a cross between a crocodile and a toothed whale, scientists were unable to agree what kind of animal it was. It was, however, re-created as a crocodile-like animal. Known as the Beast of Maastricht, it was stolen by Napoleon's troops in 1795 and put on display at an exhibition in Paris.

Then, some time later, a twelve-year-old girl by the name of Mary Anning, whilst looking for sea shells in Dorset, came across a 12-foot-long fossil. As it looked like the skeleton of a giant lizard, it was named Icthyosaurus, meaning 'fish lizard'. Mary Anning continued, through adult-hood, to collect fossils with her family, and made a living out of selling them to scientists for sending off to museums.

It was not until 1842 that the British public first came across the word 'dinosaur', when scientist, Robert Owen, invented the word 'dinosauria', meaning 'terrible lizards' for these fossils in order to distinguish them from the living reptiles known at that time. He went on to create his own concept of the dinosaur and supervised their modelling for putting on display at The Great Exhibition of 1851, held at The Crystal Palace. This display of life-sized dinosaurs, set in appropriate looking landscapes, attracted thousands of spectators, and was the first theme park in the world to be opened.

The models of Dan yr Ogof are made of fibre glass and have been crafted by Mr Derek Collam of Scunthorpe. As large as they are, they arrive by road on low-loaders and are put into position by helicopter. There are always anxious moments when something of this size and weight is lowered into such a confined space, and on one occasion, a 25ft dinosaur weighing half a ton swayed precariously from the Jetranger helicopter. But whilst the pilot kept the machine steady, a cargo man gave assistance and the half a ton model was placed into its new position without damage.

Without a doubt, the great family of dinosaurs is extremely popular with visitors of all ages and now forms an integral part of the entire Complex with their roars rising above the trees and providing an atmospheric dimension to the area.

The park has not been without its drama. One spring, birds looking for a place to nest found the mouth of the Tyrannosaurus Rex an ideal nesting place. At the time, the model was encased in scaffolding for its usual spring-clean, and Mini, the owner's cat, seeing the birds flying in and out, found her way up and entered the model. Once inside, she found herself trapped for two days behind the teeth. Visitors, on hearing the cat's plaintiff cries, alerted the Management and threw scraps of food her way. After a couple of attempts to rescue Mini by a ski instructor and a caving expert had failed, Mr Ashford Price's son James, who was then a schoolboy, was slim enough to wriggle inside the monster's mouth and, with the aid of a rope, climbed down to bring out the completely unharmed Mini.

Today, the Tyrannosaurus Rex, standing up to its full height, does not appear to intimidate the children. They are seen to mingle freely among the giants, completely enthralled by the magic they generate. In fact, on taking a closer look, each dinosaur seems to have acquired its own particular personality. It is no wonder, that, on arriving back down the hill, the children steer their parents in the direction of the Souvenir Shop where they can choose a tiny replica of their favourite one from the wide selection available.

Such scenes of delight have made the entire development all the more worthwhile, having ensured that every child and adult has enjoyed a visit they will long remember.

Other Outside Attractions:

Ski Slope

A Ski Slope, 200 feet long and 168 feet high, was constructed on the side of the mountain in 1984, to provide all year round activity and encourage more visitors into the area. As a joint venture with the Wales Tourist Board, the workforce had first to remove 1,200 tons of rock before perfecting the slope at a constant 15 degrees, which enables thirty skiers to participate at any one time.

The slope has been carefully constructed to blend in with the natural beauty of the surroundings, and was officially opened by Mr Pryce Edwards, Chairman of the Wales Tourist Board. It provides enormous fun for those 'brushing up' on their skiing, as well as providing 'out of season' enjoyment for the skilled. There is also a ski lift which hauls skiers, one at a time, back to the top of the slope.

It is on a summer's day that the ski slope is the most popular, with parties of senior school pupils coming from far away as Berkshire and West Sussex. Skis and boots are loaned to the participants, and as the slope has fine views of the Brecon Beacons, the occasion can also be a scenic one, with the hillside providing a pleasant resting place in between the exercises.

Shire Horse Centre

The Shire Horse Centre and Farm provide another outdoor attraction which has become exceedingly popular with visitors of all ages. The children in particular clamour to see the Shire horses in their respective stalls.

Next to the stables is the Smithy, with a model of the blacksmith hard at work. It would appear that a chicken had decided to take up residence in a corner.

Next door is an excellent re-construction of the Morgan Brothers' late Victorian kitchen with authentic furniture of the period, including a Welsh Dresser. Standing among the neat rows of plates is an oil lamp which was used before the advent of electricity, and, as we sometimes found, our relatives often had the odd medicine bottle ready to hand, and these are also seen on the dresser.

In the homely scene, one of the occupants is seen sitting beside the fire, reading his newspaper. Beside him is his faithful sheep dog, Twm, who relates the story of a day on the farm. On the table is bread, and a large hunk of cheese similar to the large 2 lbs. piece which was usually included on the weekly shopping list.

Next to the kitchen is another colourful reconstruction, showing the typical Village Shop at around the turn of the Nineteenth Century with household items that many of us have long forgotten such as Lion Black Lead for blacking the iron grates which were found in every kitchen of that era; Sunlight Soap which came in bright cartons, and Nuttall's Mintoes sweets which were sold in tins. Strings of onions hanging from a hook help to create a realistic picture, as do the Welsh cakes on display along with a plucked chicken, eggs, loaves of bread, and joints of meat.

Again, Twm is there to relate the story and tells us how Megan, the young assistant, has fallen asleep on her job.

A charming tableau of one of the farmers feeding a lamb completes the set of Farmhouse scenes, all of which were the handiwork of a theatrical set designer from Cardiff, and all adding to the interest which is found on this lower meadow with the stone-built farmhouse providing an attractive feature to the whole area.

On 'the Farm', sheep graze contentedly with the highland cattle, oblivious of people passing by, as do the goats, horses, pigs and even a lama or two. An ostrich can also be seen strutting freely amongst the animals with ducks and geese wandering away from the pond which also provides a picturesque focal point.

Alongside the Farm, in a converted stone barn, is the **Owls' Playground**, where the younger children can play safely in the event of rain. Should that be the case, the caves are the driest place to be, making Dan yr Ogof an all season and all weather entertainment centre.

Monuments from the Past

Towards the close of 1999, more than 50 large stones were used to create summer and winter circles and an avenue connecting the two, as part of Dan yr Ogof's celebration for the coming new Millennium. The stones, which had come from a quarry near Neath and weighed 9 tons each, stand about 6 feet high.

In the meadow to the right of the entrance and leading to the Farm, is the Circle to mark the midsummer solstice. To make sure that the centre stone was placed in the exact spot where the first rays of the midsummer sun appeared, members of Dan yr Ogof's staff were there at 4 a.m. at the dawning of midsummer's day, to make sure that it was. As an added interest to visitors, white paint now marks the precise spot where the sun first struck the stone.

The circle is also the burial place of one of the Bronze Age skeletons which had been discovered in the Bone Cave. At a specially devised service, attended by the children from Penycae County Primary School, the bones were carried by Mr Ashford Price in an oblong box that had been draped with the Welsh national flag.

At the end of the funeral service, an enormous slab of rock was lowered gently over the grave and it is now a permanent tombstone for the cave dweller who had died three thousand years ago. Buried with the remains was a Time Capsule containing information about the end of the Twentieth century, with items such as postage stamps, coins, a daily newspaper and a copy of the current *Radio Times*. Also buried for future generations to discover were a school uniform and recorded interviews which the children had conducted with the senior citizens of the village.

Also attending was Mr Rhodri Morgan of the Welsh Assembly, who became its First Minister. A television crew from the BBC was on hand to record this unusual event, which was then televised on the evening's National News.

Another circle, marking the winter solstice, can be seen from the roadway leading up to the main buildings, and this is located in the top meadow. In ancient times, a line or avenue of standing stones acted as a kind of signpost which guided the traveller directly to the Circles, and this has also been faithfully reproduced at Dan yr Ogof.

Not far away, on the Cribarth, is an avenue of seven stones called Saithmaen which had been erected in prehistoric times to mark the track across the ridge of the mountain, with another set of stones leading the traveller down to a small circle at the bottom. This circle is comprised of twenty-one stones and has a large red sandstone standing in its centre. In the vicinity are the remains of hut circles and a cairn which is known locally as Bedd-y-Cawr (Grave of the Giant). Locally, the Cribarth is known as **The Sleeping Giant**. Its silhouette looks like a man lying down. Legend has it that it is Prince Llewellyn, resting until he is called to come to the aid of the Welsh people at time of need.

Stone Circles first appeared on the British landscape between 2,500–1,800 BC and have always been surrounded in mystery. Without documentation, one can only guess that they were places where tribal rituals and other ceremonies were carried out at certain times of the year, either for worship, or, even more sinisterly, where human sacrifices were carried out.

More than one thousand prehistoric circles were built in Ireland and Britain, and were regarded as sacred places. The most renowned of these circles, or henges, is, without doubt, Stonehenge, whose circle, it was discovered, had been planned to line up with the midsummer sunrise.

The macabre theory that circles had been used for human sacrifices arose when burials of women and children were found inside Stonehenge's two entrances. Human jaw bones were also discovered in the surrounding ditch of the circle situated at Avebury in Wiltshire; and the burnt bones of children were also found in the middle of a Druids' Circle in North Wales. Another site where human remains have been found is at Loanhead of Daviot in Aberdeenshire. There, in its centre, was a pit containing fragments of children's skulls.

The most notable circle in Wales is located at Penmaen Mawr. This was documented in a wash drawing made by an artist touring Wales in 1774 and is now in the National Library of Wales. The monument was described as having 'ten upright stones of equal distances between them' with the largest being 'eight feet three inches' high. The diameter of the circle was measured as eighty feet.

There is also a small circle at Gors Fawr, in Pembrokeshire, situated within sight of the Preseli Hills, from where the famous blue stone for Stonehenge was quarried.

These Stone Circles inspired the idea of creating bardic circles, or *Gorseddau*, to mark the sites of the annual National Eisteddfod of Wales, and they provide an attractive feature to many towns and villages where the Eisteddfod has taken place. The nearest one is at Ystradgynlais.

Burial Monuments

Also at Dan yr Ogof is an example of an ancient burial chamber which consists of a large slab of stone placed on some upright ones. These were usually covered over with earth and stones to protect the corpse, but many with just the single slab resting on supporting stones have been discovered throughout Wales and are known as cromlechs. They were well designed to enable the lesser stones to support the weight of the larger one and vary from two supporting stones to three or four. Such was their design, that it was first thought they were altars on which human sacrifices had been carried out. As they became part of the Welsh landscape, they were well documented by visiting eighteenth century painters.

One of the best examples is Arthur's Stone, at Cefn Bryn, near Swansea, and the enormous cromlech at Gwernvale, near Crickhowel, was also portrayed on canvas. Both paintings can be seen at The National Museum of Wales.

It transpired that on opening one of these burial chambers at Llanarmon-yn-Iâl, Clwyd, several urns containing ashes were found, including several of the occupant's larger bones which had not entirely burnt.

Evidence that Neolithic man favoured these monuments as burial chambers has been found throughout Wales. They are called Portal Dolmens and are different from the cromlechs because they have a passage leading into the burial chamber with another large slab placed at the entrance.

A significant number of these tombs have been found in Breconshire, particularly around the Talgarth area, and one, excavated at Tŷ Isaf by Professor Grimes, had several chambers and passages. Inside was a large number of well-fired bowls with fluted rims. In dating this pottery to Middle Neolithic times, the tomb was built sometime between 3200–2800 BC.

During the 1st century, AD 800-1000, another significant monument appeared in the form of a single pillar of rock with a cross carved within a circle and was the first symbol of Christianity to appear on the landscape. These Celtic crosses often appeared as landmarks. Many contained inscriptions in Latin and were richly decorated. Some were located at churches. The National Museum in Cardiff has a large selection of these monuments from different parts of Wales and they provide an impressive display. Among them is a stone pillar which contains the earliest form of Anglo-Saxon decoration in bright red and green. Much of its original colour has survived to this date

This kind of decoration first came to Wales when the Vikings began raiding the monastries in Northumbria and along the coastline of the Irish Sea, forcing the men who maintained these monuments to escape. Some came to Wales bringing their artistic designs with them. They survive to this date with modern-day artists casting them in silver and other metals into objects of adornment.

These monuments from the past are our link with those people who began applying their skills, from sharpening flint to creating bronze, and then going on to produce iron objects of great beauty. This was the age of mysterious rituals, of curious myths, and the birth of Celtic legends.

In Wales, the mountains dominate our landscape and have been an integral part of our lives. The treasures found at Dan yr Ogof make us wonder what others lie within their heart.

Visiting archeologists have unearthed many interesting sites which link us to our historic past. Mortimer Wheeler once wrote: 'The hills of Wales teem with the vestiges of early man...' In the Upper Swansea Valley that has certainly proved to be the case. We wonder what else there is to find.